KNOWLEDGE ACQUISITION: SELECTED RESEARCH AND COMMENTARY

edited by

SANDRA MARCUS

Boeing Computer Services
Seattle, Washington

A Special Issue of Machine Learning on Knowledge Acquisition

Reprinted from Machine Learning
Vol. 4, Nos. 3–4 (1989)

KLUWER ACADEMIC PUBLISHERS
BOSTON/DORDRECHT/LONDON

ISBN 0–7923–9062–8

Distributors for North America:
Kluwer Academic Publishers
101 Philip Drive
Assinippi Park
Norwell, MA 02061
U.S.A.

Distributors for all other countries:
Kluwer Academic Publishers Group
Distribution Centre
Post Office Box 322
3300 AH Dordrecht
THE NETHERLANDS

Printed in The Netherlands

KNOWLEDGE ACQUISITION: SELECTED RESEARCH AND COMMENTARY
A Special Issue of Machine Learning on Knowledge Acquisition

Machine Learning 4, 247–249 (1989)
© 1989 Kluwer Academic Publishers, Boston. Manufactured in The Netherlands.

Introduction: A Sampler in Knowledge Acquisition for the Machine Learning Community

This special issue is devoted to invited editorials and technical papers on knowledge acquisition. In the past, special issues have been devoted to recognized subfields of machine learning, where a subfield might be characterized by a particular method of machine learning, such as genetic algorithms. The relationship between machine learning and knowledge acquisition is not so clearcut as the field-subfield one. Neither are the methods of knowledge acquisition so homogeneous and easily characterized as for genetic algorithms.

Just as with machine learning as a whole, people who consider themselves to be working in the field of knowledge acquisition are identified more by the goal of their work than by any particular methodology they apply. I think most of us in knowledge acquisition would agree that our goal is to make expert systems easier to build and maintain and, along the way, to make the expert systems built more explainable, more robust, and so on. This aim has given the knowledge acquisition field an engineering flavor. Our tools and methodologies are judged by their suitability for their user community and the environment in which they are used, and by the performance of the knowledge bases they produce and the expert systems they support. We tend to place a heavy emphasis on fielding systems and evaluating the practicality of our approaches.

In the quest for this goal, knowledge acquisition workers have employed a diversity of methods. Some work in knowledge acquisition, including some of the earliest work, was done using traditional machine learning techniques (e.g. [Michalski and Chilausky, 1980; Quinlan, 1986]), but other knowledge acquisition approaches fall outside of what is generally viewed as machine learning. In general, machine learning techniques are appreciated in the knowledge acquisition field only according to their ability to achieve practical results. In turn, the machine learning community seems to show little interest in tools or methodologies that have great practical benefits to today's expert systems but don't exhibit "real" learning.

In part, a goal of this issue is to extend a hand from the knowledge acquisition community to the machine learning community. To a large degree, knowledge acquisition and machine learning share a common goal: We are each trying to improve the performance of some automated system. Knowledge acquisition is very eager to use what it can from machine learning. It is both rewarding and challenging to put one's work into practice—even more challenging as we raise our ambitions for the performance of our application systems. We hope you'll accept the challenge, or at least keep it in mind. Furthermore, because of our shared goal, we have encountered and will continue to encounter some of the same problems. Issues such as appropriateness of domain models, design of lexicons for exchange between teacher and pupil, credit assignment in debugging, and sources and use of bias cut across both fields. Work in either community can reveal issues and approaches that should be of interest to the other community, even when the results are not directly importable.

What follows is a sampler of work in knowledge acquisition. It comprises three technical papers and six guest editorials. The technical papers give an in-depth look at some of the important issues and current approaches in knowledge acquisition. The editorials were produced by authors who were basically invited to sound off. I've tried to group and order the contributions somewhat coherently. The following annotations emphasize the connections among the separate pieces.

Buchanan's editorial starts on the theme of "Can machine learning offer anything to expert systems?" He emphasizes the practical goals of knowledge acquisition and the challenge of aiming for them.

Lenat's editorial briefly describes experience in the development of CYC that straddles both fields. He outlines a two-phase development that relies on an engineering approach early on and aims for a crossover to more automated techniques as the size of the knowledge base increases.

Bareiss, Porter, and Murray give the first technical paper. It comes from a laboratory of machine learning researchers who have taken an interest in supporting the development of knowledge bases, with an emphasis on how development changes with the growth of the knowledge base. The paper describes two systems. The first, Protos, adjusts the training it expects and the assistance it provides as its knowledge grows. The second, KI, is a system that helps integrate knowledge into an already very large knowledge base. It is designed to help acquire knowledge at the fringes of a knowledge base built using the CYC knowledge-base editing tools.

Clancey's editorial reflects on the enterprise of building expert systems. He debunks a popular myth about the nature of knowledge and provides a thoughtful perspective on the goals and challenges of the knowledge acquisition process.

Gruber's is the second technical paper of the collection. He analyzes the problems of knowledge acquisition in terms of representation mismatch, taking up some of the modeling themes in Clancey's editorial. These ideas are applied in the development of ASK, an interactive knowledge acquisition tool that elicits strategic knowledge from people. He defines strategic knowledge to be that knowledge used by an agent to decide what action to perform next, where actions have consequences external to the agent.

McDermott's editorial focuses on the aim of one particular line of work in knowledge acquisition—one that makes use of task-specific architectures. The practical aim is conveyed in the title: "The World Would Be a Better Place if Non-Programmers Could Program."

Chandra's editorial also explores the issue of how task-specific architectures support knowledge acquisition and emphasizes the connection to machine learning approaches as well. He supports his ideas with a description of some recent work in the OSU Generic Tasks group.

Musen's is the final technical paper. His work embraces the aim that McDermott describes—that is, to provide a tool that allows non-programmers to program. He places his work in the framework of constructing and extending domain models. This paper describes PROTÉGÉ, and interactive knowledge-acquisition system that addresses the two activities individually.

Finally, Boose and Gaines' editorial comments on the state-of-the-art in knowledge acquisition, based on their experience as the organizers of a series of workshops on the subject. It gives a little flavor of the variety of work being done in knowledge acquisition, but emphasizes the development of interactive knowledge acquisition tools. For those interested in more information on knowledge acquisition, their editorial concludes by listing sources of information on past workshops and by announcing future events.

References

Michalski, R.S., and Chilausky, R.L. 1980. Learning by being told and learning from examples: An experimental comparison of the two methods of knowledge acquisition in the context of developing an expert system for soybean disease diagnosis. *Policy Analysis and Information Systems*, 4. 125–160.

Quinlan, J.R. 1986. Induction of decision trees. *Machine Learning*, 1. 81–106.

—Sandra Marcus
Advanced Technology Center
Boeing Computer Services

Machine Learning, 4, 251–254 (1989)

Can Machine Learning Offer Anything to Expert Systems?

BRUCE G. BUCHANAN
Professor of Computer Science, Medicine, and Philosophy, University of Pittsburgh, Pittsburgh, PA 15260

Today's expert systems have no ability to learn from experience. This commonly heard criticism, unfortunately, is largely true. Except for simple classification systems, expert systems do not employ a learning component to construct parts of their knowledge bases from libraries of previously solved cases. And none that I know of couples learning into closed-loop modification based on experience, although the SOAR architecture [Rosenbloom and Newell 1985] comes the closest to being the sort of integrated system needed for continuous learning. Learning capabilities are needed for intelligent systems that can remain useful in the face of changing environments or changing standards of expertise. Why are the learning methods we know how to implement not being used to build or maintain expert systems in the commercial world?

Part of the answer lies in the syntactic view we have traditionally taken toward learning. Statistical techniques such as linear regression, for example, are "knowledge-poor" procedures that are unable to use knowledge we may bring to the learning task. However, learning is a problem-solving activity. As such, we can and should analyze the requirements and functional specifications, the input and output, and the assumptions and limitations. If there is one thing we have learned in AI it is that complex, i.e., combinatorially explosive and ill-structured, problems often can be tamed by introducing knowledge into an otherwise syntactic procedure.

There is not a single model for learning effectively, as is confirmed by the proliferation of methods, just as there is not a single model of diagnosis or of scheduling. If the machine learning community is going to make a difference in the efficiency of building commercial expert systems, we need not only more methods but a better understanding of the criteria for deciding which method best suits which learning problem. No matter what model one adopts, there is a significant chance of success in coupling a learning program with an expert system. And there will be significant benefits to the machine learning community in terms of research problems that crystallize out of the solution of applications.

The workhorse of knowledge acquisition for commercial expert systems is still knowledge engineering. It is labor intensive and prone to error because it involves discussions among persons with very different backgrounds. We are slightly better at teaching knowledge engineering, and practicing it, than we were a decade ago. It has the outstanding virtue that it works. Partly because it is slow, it also allows more deliberate examination of conceptual frameworks, of assumptions, and of mistakes. But it is too slow: it stands in the same relation to knowledge acquisition as do paper and pencil to calculation.

Speeding up the knowledge engineering process has led to the development of customized editors of the SALT variety [Marcus and McDermott 1989]. These are being used successfully and provide some assistance to knowledge base developers. But they are not learning programs; they are editors. As an aside, though, they allow us to meet McCarthy's 1958 challenge [McCarthy 1958] of building programs that can accept advice before we build systems that learn on their own. In a customized editor we see elements of expert systems. They use knowledge of a generic task such as diagnosis to guide the acquisition and debugging of a knowledge base. With our increased experience in building systems over the last decade, we should now be able to integrate the techniques of TEIRESIAS [Davis 1982] and ROGET [Bennett 1985] for even more powerful editors.

As we move closer to automated knowledge acquisition and away from knowledge engineering, we must understand better how to convey the built-in assumptions of the programs that assist in constructing knowledge bases. With expert systems, there is a potential danger that the designers of programs will have different conceptual frameworks in mind than the users. In the case of learning programs, the same potential danger arises in the mismatch of frameworks between the designers of the learning programs and the designers of the expert systems. We in the machine learning community have not adequately addressed this question, nor would we think of it unless there were a pressing need to apply machine learning techniques to problems of interest to another community.

Inductive learning has received considerable attention since the 1950s, with several approaches now in our growing toolkit of programs that can assist in knowledge acquisition. Some programs assume the data are correct, that the descriptions and classifications of examples are error-free; some of the same ones assume that the examples are all available at once, and hereafter remain available; others assume that classification rules are categorical; most assume that the rules to be learned are one-step conjunctive rules. Successful applications of ID3 and C4 [Quinlan, et al. 1986] and their cousins have provided knowledge bases for working expert systems whose task is to classify. These, together with a few other isolated cases of an expert system being built with the assistance of a learning program, have kept alive the promise of payoff from the 35-year investment in learning research.

Explanation-based learning (EBL) is now receiving even more attention than induction or similarity-based learning. Here, more than with induction, the problem-solving nature of acquiring new knowledge is apparent. (See, for example, [Mitchell 1986].) Its main assumption is that enough theory exists to provide a rationalization of why one instance is or is not a prototypical member of a class. What else? Does it have to be a formal, deductive rationalization, or will an empirical argument suffice? (See [Smith, et al. 1985] for an argument that a weaker, empirical model will suffice.) Unfortunately, EBL has not found any applications in building expert systems, thus it is still demonstrated only in laboratory prototypes.

Case-based and analogical reasoning are still pipe dreams when matched against the harsh standards of robustness of commercial applications. Some of the problems stem from the dilemma that we can find some mappings from any previous case or previously studied domain to the present one: we almost have to know the answer in order to find the case or the analogy that lets us program a machine to find the answer. Analogical reasoning involves at least two problem-solving steps: finding a useful analogous domain (or object or process) and finding relevant mappings between the analog and the original thing. It is not a robust method in the sense that it still produces too many false positive results. Moreover, we don't see many suggestions for making these methods more selective. Their power seems to lie in offering suggestions when we have run out of other ideas.

What about neural nets? They certainly are popular because the idea of getting something for nothing has always held great appeal. They have shown some success in knowledge-poor tasks, such as character recognition and other perceptual tasks. Expert systems, by their very nature, are knowledge-intensive, however, and thus are less amenable to learning with syntactic reinforcement methods. Once a neural net is tuned, there is no way to understand why it succeeds on some cases and fails on others except to say that the weights on some nodes are higher than on others. Moreover, their construction is not free; considerable effort must be invested in laying out the structure of the network before examples can be presented.

Only a few of the techniques in the literature are immediately useful, and these have their limits. Part of our research charge needs to include understanding the scope and limits of different methods and determining when they are applicable. Expert systems provide a strong rationale for continued funding of research on machine learning, but they also serve to sharpen our understanding of problems.

Expert systems offer a focus for development of new machine learning methods and better understanding of old ones. Of course, we need basic research as well as demand-driven research. At the moment, however, there is an imbalance in the amount of work on learning in domains where we do not need to learn and on techniques with crippling assumptions. Let us attempt to understand the context of the commercial, military, and medical needs. In research on machine learning, as on other problem-solving methods, new wrinkles— perhaps new opportunities—will arise in experimenting with real, complex knowledge bases and applications.

Using an expert system as a testbed offers a tough test of success. The commercial world of expert systems at large seems unconvinced that machine learning has anything to offer yet. I strongly disagree. Inductive learning, at least, is already in limited use, and present methods can be extended to make them more useful. Some of the issues that need to be resolved in order to make inductive methods a mainstay of commercial knowledge acquisition are already modestly well understood: learning in the context of noisy and uncertain data, exploiting an existing partial theory, representing the objects of learning in a form other than classification rules, and tailoring the learning to the specific context in which the learned information will be used. These are partly issues of utility, but they are important research problems as well. Machine learning is ready for development now, with attendant benefits to us in crystallizing current and new research problems.

References

Bennett, J.S. 1985. ROGET: A knowledge-based system for acquiring the conceptual structure of a diagnostic expert system. *J. Automated Reasoning 1*, 49–74.

Davis, R. 1982. TEIRESIAS: Applications of meta-level knowledge. In R. Davis and D. Lenat (Eds.). 1982. *Knowledge-based systems in artificial intelligence*. New York: McGraw-Hill.

Marcus, S. and McDermott, J. 1989. SALT: A knowledge acquisition language for propose-and-revise systems. *Artificial Intelligence 39*, 1–37.

McCarthy, J. 1968. Programs with common sense. *Proc. Symposium on the Mechanisation of Thought Processes.* Reprinted in M. Minsky (Ed.), *Semantic Information Processing.* Cambridge, MA: MIT Press, 1968.

Mitchell, T.M., Keller, R., and Kedar-Cabelli, S. 1986. Explanation-based generalization: A unifying view. *Machine Learning 1*, 47–80.

Quinlan, J.R., Compton, P.J., Horn, K.A., and Lazarus, L. 1986. Inductive knowledge acquisiton: A case study. *Proceedings Second Australian Conference on Applications of Expert Systems.* In J.R. Quinlan (Ed.), *Applications of Expert Systems.* Maidenhead: Academic Press (in press).

Rosenbloom, P.S., and Newell, A. 1985. The chunking of goal hierarchies: A generalized model of practice. In R. Michalski, J. Carbonell, and T. Mitchell (Eds.), *Machine learning: An artificial intelligence approach (Vol. 2).* Los Altos, CA: Morgan-Kaufmann.

Smith, R.G., Winston, H., Mitchell, T., and Buchanan, B.G. 1985. Representation and use of explicit justification for knowledge base refinement. In *Proceedings of IJCAI85.* Los Altos, CA: Morgan-Kaufmann.

Machine Learning, 4, 255–257 (1989)

When Will Machines Learn?

DOUGLAS B. LENAT
Principal Scientist and Director of AI, MCC, 3500 West Balcones Center Drive, Austin, Texas 78759

Why don't our learning programs just keep on going and become generally intelligent? The source of the problem is that most of our learning occurs at the fringe of what we already know. The more you know, the more (and faster) you can learn.

Unfortunately, fringe (analogical) reasoning is frequently employed purely as a dramatic device. For example, a news reporter talks about a child's valiant battle against disease; or a government issues a clinical-sounding report of a military containment and sterilization operation. This use obscures the fact that analogical reasoning is a critical component of human intelligence; it can help discover new concepts (e.g., is there a military analogue of vaccination? is there a medical analogue of propaganda?) and help flesh them out, as well as helping us to cope with novel situations.

The inverse of "the more your know. . ." is the real culprit: not knowing much implies slow learning. Even the largest machine learning programs (e.g., Eurisko) know only a tiny, tiny fraction of what even a six-year-old child knows ($10**4$ things versus $10**9$ things). So Learning is fueled by Knowledge, and human-scale learning demands a human-scale amount of knowledge. I see two ways to get it:

1. The 100% Natural Approach: Figure out all the instincts, skills, needs, drives, and predispositions to learning that Nature (Evolution, God, . . .) has hard-wired into human brains and spinal cords and sense organs, and figure out how neonates' raw perception refines into usable knowledge. Then build such a system incorporating all of those things, plus, of course, the right sort of "body" and allow it to "live" for years in the real world: nurture it, let it play, let it bump into walls, teach it to talk, let it go to kindergarten, etc.
2. The Prime the Pump Approach: Codify, in one immense knowledge base, the tens of millions of facts, algorithms, heuristics, stories, representations, etc., that "everybody knows"—the things that the writer of a newspaper article can safely assume that the reader already knows (consensus reality knowledge).

Once the large consensus reality knowledge base exists, either via methodology (1) or (2), then the everyday sort of fringe learning takes over, and the system should be educable in the usual ways: by giving it carefully graded series of readings to do, asking it thought-provoking questions, and helping it over novel or difficult parts by posing a good metaphor drawn from its existing knowledge base.

There are many researchers who are working on limited forms of approach (1)—e.g., the CMU World Modeling Project—and approach (2)—e.g., the Stanford KSL Engineering Design Project.

The CYC project, which Mary Shepherd and I have been working on at MCC since late 1984, is aiming at the fully scaled-up approach (2). We knew when we started that we would have to overcome many representation thorns (e.g., how to deal with time, space, belief, awareness, causality, emotion, stuffs, etc.) and methodological thorns (e.g., how to have tons of knowledge enterers simultaneously editing the same KB, and how to keep their semantics from diverging).

Overcoming those thorns meant finding an adequate way to handle the 99% of the common cases that crop up in everyday life. For example, CYC only represents pieces of time that can be expressed using a simple grammar; those pieces of time are interrelated using a set of 50 relations (such as ends-during) derived by R.V. Guha. We have developed two dozen specialized inference methods (such as inheritance, automatic classification, slot-value subsumption, Horn clause rules) rather than having a system that relies on one general inference procedure. CYC can't easily represent or reason about "the Cantor set of moments from three to four p.m.'—but then again, neither can most people! Time and again, that pragmatic focus (not always scruffy, by the way) has pulled us through. Lenat and Guha [1988] describes the CYC project in great detail and explains our solutions to each thorn.

Since 1984, we've been building and organizing and reorganizing our growing consensus reality KB in CYC. We now have about half a million entries in it, and we expect it to increase by one order of magnitude by mid-1990 and one more by the end of 1994. We expect that at roughly that point, a kind of crossover will occur, and it will be cost-effective to enlarge the system from that point onward by having it learn mostly on its own and from online texts.

Naturally, we must build up the CYC KB from some sort of primitives. We have assumed that it must be built from deeply understood knowledge rather than from complex "impenetrable" predicates (or slots or whatever). That is, you can't have LaysEggsInWater unless you also have eggs, water, and so on. At first, doing this just made life difficult; having a deep but small KB didn't pay off. Yet, fortunately, when we began to build CYC ever larger and larger, we found that the set of primitives began to converge. That is, it requires less and less work to enter each new fact. This phenomenon is not surprising (it was, e.g., predicted in Pat Hayes' [1985] Naive Physics Manifesto). Still, it was quite comforting to see it really happen!

What would divergence look like? One knowledge enterer might use another's already-entered terms to mean slightly different things. Or they might re-enter some knowledge that was already entered in the system under a different name. Thanks to an array of explicit and implicit methods for stating and enforcing semantics, the KB appears to be converging, not diverging.

One key to preventing divergence, much in the spirit of Jim Bennett's ROGET system, is having CYC itself actively help with its own continuing enlargement. For example, CYC brings its full KB to bear to help make guesses during the frame-copy&edit process, to help detect subtle conflicts and errors in the KB, to find analogies that turn out to be different individuals encoding the same knowledge in multiple ways, and to notice gaps and asymmetries in its KB.

So, in summary, you could say that we've chosen an engineering approach to getting a large initial KB. The various representation and methodology thorns have been faced up to and trimmed back; they have neither been avoided nor fixated upon.

Manual KB-building activity is not considered part of machine learning, so it may appear that I've disowned the ML field. Not so! The absence of a CYC-like consensus reality KB is the major bottleneck to automated knowledge acquisition. (Incidentally, I also believe that the same absence is holding back progress in other areas, such as the semantics part of natural language understanding or getting expert systems to be less brittle and to cooperate with each other.)

I was invited to write this paper because my 1975–1984 work on AM and Eurisko helped to spark the rebirth of the machine learning field. I fully expect that CYC will spark a vastly greater renaissance in that field, and that I will be rehabilitated (considered a learning researcher again) during the latter half of the 1990s.

As a parting shot, let me remark that since CYC started in September, 1984, and the crossover to automated KA was and still is scheduled to occur ten years later than that, a tongue-in-cheek answer to this editorial's apparently rhetorical title (When Will Machines Learn?) might be: "September 1, 1994."

References

Hayes, P. 1985. Naive physics manifesto. In Hobbs and Moore (Eds.), *Formal theories of the common sense world*. Norwood: Ablex.

Lenat, D., and Guha, R.V. 1988. The world according to CYC. (MCC Technical Report Number ACA-AI-300-88.) An expanded version of this, in book form, is (in press) *Building large knowledge-based systems: Representation and inference in the CYC project*. Addison-Wesley.

Machine Learning, 4, 259-283 (1989)

Supporting Start-to-Finish Development of Knowledge Bases

RAY BAREISS   BAREISS@VUSE.VANDERBILT.EDU
Computer Science Department, Vanderbilt University, Nashville, TN 37235

BRUCE W. PORTER   PORTER@CS.UTEXAS.EDU
KENNETH S. MURRAY   MURRAY@CS.UTEXAS.EDU
Computer Sciences Department, University of Texas, Austin, TX 78712

Abstract. Developing knowledge bases using knowledge-acquisition tools is difficult because each stage of development requires performing a distinct knowledge-acquisition task. This paper describes these different tasks and surveys current tools that perform them. It also addresses two issues confronting tools for start-to-finish development of knowledge bases. The first issue is how to support multiple stages of development. This paper describes Protos, a knowledge-acquisition tool that adjusts the training it expects and assistance it provides as its knowledge grows. The second issue is how to integrate new information into a large knowledge base. This issue is addressed in the description of a second tool, KI, that evaluates new information to determine its consequences for existing knowledge.

Key words: knowledge-acquisition tools, knowledge-base refinement, knowledge-base development

1. Introduction

The purpose of a knowledge-acquisition tool is to help with *knowledge-base development—* the progression of a knowledge base from a level of complete ignorance to a desired level of knowledge. Supporting start-to-finish development is hard because different stages of development require different forms of assistance. In this paper we describe the support that current knowledge-acquisition methods provide, issues in supporting start-to-finish development, and specific tools we have built to study these issues.

Developing a knowledge base typically involves three stages: elicitation, refinement, and reformulation. During elicitation, the basic terminology and conceptual structure of the knowledge base is acquired. During refinement, knowledge is added to the skeletal structure and debugged. Finally, during reformulation, the knowledge base is optimized for problem solving.

Knowledge-acquisition tasks have been defined for each stage of development. For example, a task during knowledge refinement is to explain how a faulty conclusion was reached so that the knowledge base can be debugged. Section 2 describes the tasks required for each stage of development and surveys knowledge-acquisition tools that perform these tasks.

To support start-to-finish development, knowledge-acquisition tools must do more than sequentially perform these tasks. In addition to performing the tasks required for each stage of development, the knowledge needed to perform successive knowledge-acquisition tasks must be acquired. For example, during systematic elicitation, the justification for inferences should be acquired so that conclusions can be explained during knowledge refinement.

13

Requiring such stage-setting complicates developing knowledge bases with a single tool or a collection of tools.

Our research addresses two issues confronting tools for start-to-finish development of large-scale knowledge bases. The first issue is spanning multiple stages of development, which requires versatility to meet the needs of each stage. Ideally, transitions between stages are seamless, and there are no gaps in support during development. Section 3 describes Protos, which adjusts the problem-solving assistance it provides and the training it expects as the knowledge base develops. Its ability to support start-to-finish development is empirically demonstrated; through direct interaction with a domain expert, Protos has achieved proficiency at diagnosing hearing disorders and continues to learn as it is used.

The second issue is integrating new information into existing knowledge. *Knowledge integration* involves evaluating new information to determine its consequences for existing knowledge. For example, new information might conflict with existing knowledge or reveal gaps in the knowledge base. Although knowledge integration is performed throughout development, our research focuses on automating the task during the advanced stages of development. This focus identifies the knowledge required to perform the task, which is critical to its application. Section 4 discusses our current research on KI, a tool for knowledge integration that efficiently determines nonsuperficial consequences of new information.

2. The Tasks and Tools of Knowledge-Base Development

In general, there are three stages in developing a knowledge base:

- During systematic elicitation, the basic terminology and conceptual structure of the knowledge base is acquired.
- During knowledge refinement, the knowledge base is debugged and extended.
- During knowledge reformulation, the knowledge base is compiled to solve problems more efficiently.

Sections 2.1 through 2.3 describe these stages and survey knowledge-acquisition tools supporting each stage.

An ideal tool supports all stages of development. When there is little problem-solving knowledge available, the tool interviews the domain expert to acquire basic information. As the knowledge base grows, the tool helps identify gaps and inconsistencies responsible for problem-solving failures. Finally, the tool solves problems and improves performance without explicit training.

A "workbench of tools" approximates the ideal tool. The workbench organizes a collection of tools, each of which helps with a particular development phase. As discussed in Section 2.4, this method differs from the ideal tool in that the support it offers is not continuous. Moreover, many current tools are not good candidates for the workbench because they do not set the stage for the tools used after them. In order to compare research results, much of this discussion focuses on knowledge acquisition tools for heuristic classification. Heuristic classification is the predominant problem-solving method in current expert systems

[Clancey, 1985]. The method relates the features describing a problem to a predetermined set of solutions and is useful for a broad range of tasks, such as diagnosis, that require classifying an unknown object or situation.

2.1. Systematic Elicitation

The primary task during systematic elicitation is acquiring the conceptual structure of a knowledge base through a structured interview with the domain expert. The conceptual structure is a "description of the kinds of domain-specific inferences that the consultant will perform and the facts that will support these inferences" [Bennett, 1985]. For heuristic classification, this includes the predetermined set of solutions and the features that describe problems. Researchers believe elicitation of the conceptual structure must be systematic in order to prod the domain expert's memory and to avoid overlooking elements of the conceptual structure.

The knowledge required to perform systematic elicitation is a *model* to guide interaction with the user. The model describes the important components of a knowledge base for a problem-solving method or task. Some tools use a weak model of a generic problem-solving method, such as heuristic classification. Others use a strong model of a problem-solving method specific to a particular domain, such as diagnostic reasoning for disk failures.

ETS [Boose, 1984] is representative of systematic-elicitation tools that use a weak model of classification. The ETS model contains information about the classification process, such as the use of discriminating features to select among competing classifications. The first step in using ETS is enumerating the conclusions that the knowledge-based system should be able to reach. Given these conclusions, ETS systematically elicits the conceptual structure by directing the expert through two tasks. The first task is to identify features that discriminate among conclusions. The second task is to rate each feature's importance to each conclusion. ETS uses these features and associations to construct a prototype knowledge base. Ongoing research on Aquinus [Boose and Bradshaw, 1987] focuses, in part, on refining the knowledge base by adjusting the features' importance ratings and by expanding the sets of conclusions and features.

A systematic-elicitation tool using a strong model can be more focused. Such a tool is Roget [Bennett, 1985], which acquires the conceptual structure of a knowledge base by selecting and instantiating one of several available models. For example, starting with a model of medical diagnosis manually abstracted from a previously built knowledge base, Roget interviews the domain expert for specific diagnostic categories, symptoms, test results, predisposing factors, and rules for diagnosing blood infections. Going further in strengthening the problem-solving model, Opal [Musen, Fagan, Combs, and Shortliffe, 1987] uses a model of oncology to elicit chemotherapy treatment plans. The expert communicates by completing treatment forms using domain-specific terms.

Current tools for systematic elicitation are effective during the initial stage of knowledge base development. During this stage there is insufficient domain knowledge to solve problems. The tools interview a domain expert, but ask questions unlike those typically answered by the expert. In contrast, the tools discussed next acquire knowledge during problem solving.

2.2. Knowledge Refinement

The primary task during knowledge refinement is to incrementally debug a prototype knowledge base. Unlike conventional software systems, top-down development is impractical because the specification and design of a knowledge base cannot be formalized. Researchers have taken two approaches to knowledge refinement. Static analysis scans the knowledge base for patterns that suggest weak inference paths or missing knowledge. Dynamic analysis uses the knowledge base to process a set of test cases to reveal problem-solving errors. These analysis methods focus the developer on repairs and extensions of the knowledge base.

Teiresias [Davis, 1977], which employs dynamic analysis, exemplifies tools for knowledge refinement. The domain expert presents a test case to the performance system. If the expert deems the result incorrect, Teiresias traces the erroneous reasoning path. Teiresias highlights portions of the knowledge base that may be responsible for the mistake, and the expert repairs the gap or inconsistency. As the expert introduces inference rules, Tieresias compares them with rule models abstracted from the knowledge base. Each rule model records correlations between antecedent terms and consequent terms. If a new rule violates a pattern, Teiresias reports to the domain expert and suggests a modification of the rule that conforms to the pattern. The refinement process continues until the domain expert is satisfied with the system's performance. Other knowledge-refinement systems include MORE [Kahn, Nowlan, and McDermott, 1985], which uses static analysis, and MOLE [Eshelman, Ehret, McDermott, and Tan, 1987], which combines static and dynamic analysis.

Knowledge-refinement tools use the knowledge base in two ways. First, they use the problem-solving ability of the knowledge base to identify failures. When problem solving fails, the tool elicits knowledge from the expert to advance the knowledge base's development. Second, some tools use explicit knowledge of justifications for inference rules to determine the cause of problem-solving failures [Smith, Winston, Mitchell, and Buchanan, 1985] and to explain each failure [Neches, Swartout, and Moore, 1985]. Using the knowledge base in these ways requires an initial conceptual structure capable of solving problems, revealing bugs, and explaining failures. Most tools for knowledge refinement (and systematic elicitation) do not acquire this initial knowledge.

2.3. Knowledge Reformulation

The primary task during knowledge reformulation is compiling the knowledge base for more efficient problem solving. This requires an initial knowledge base, called the domain theory, which is assumed to be complete but nonoperational. For example, the domain theory for chess encodes all the rules for play but is inefficient for selecting good chess moves.

Leap/Vexed [Mitchell, Mahadevan, and Steinberg, 1985] exemplifies tools for knowledge reformulation. This tool is an apprentice to an expert VLSI circuit designer. Vexed is given a design specification and attempts to design a circuit. If Vexed fails, then the expert provides a solution, and Leap attempts to learn from this training. First, Leap uses its pre-existing domain theory, consisting of rules of logic and primitive building blocks for logic circuits, to construct a proof that the expert's design correctly implements the specification. Then, the specification and the circuit design are generalized, subject to the constraints in the proof of correctness, to form a new design rule for Vexed's future problem solving.

Knowledge reformulation performed by Leap/Vexed is restricted by two requirements. First, the domain theory must be complete to explain every solution presented by the expert. Second, the domain theory must be strong and consistent to prove the solution is correct. Unfortunately, most domains of interest (e.g., medicine) cannot be formalized; consequently, their domain theories are incomplete, weak, and inconsistent. Additionally, knowledge-reformulation tools ignore the acquisition of the required knowledge base and address only improvements in efficiency, not in competence or explanation ability.

Integrating knowledge refinement with knowledge reformulation can address these limitations. For example, the Odysseus system [Wilkins, 1988] extends the domain theory used in knowledge reformulation. This learning apprentice observes an expert solving problems and attempts to explain the reasons underlying the expert's actions. Learning occurs when the explanation process fails. When one of the expert's actions cannot be explained, Odysseus conjectures new knowledge that would allow it to complete an explanation. The conjectured knowledge is validated by comparing it with a database of cases. If the hypothesized knowledge is consistent with the cases, it is added to the knowledge base.

2.4. Supporting Start-to-Finish Development with a Workbench of Tools

Tools for the knowledge-acquisition tasks discussed thus far support narrow phases of knowledge-base development. Conceivably, a collection of these tools could be combined into a workbench, which could support the start-to-finish development of knowledge bases. The approach is appealing, but several problems must be addressed.

The first problem with the workbench approach is that the knowledge base is rarely at a uniform level of development. For example, a knowledge base supporting heuristic classification contains inference rules relating observable data to final answers. During the knowledge base's development, parts of the knowledge base reliably classify and explain. Other parts are incomplete and erroneous. No narrow-spectrum tool from the workbench can refine the entire knowledge base. The second problem with the workbench approach is that the support it provides is not continuous. The developmental path is decomposed into discrete steps, and the consequences of supporting each step with a separate, narrow-spectrum tool can be severe:

- Mismatched knowledge representations—Each tool constructs and uses different representations for domain knowledge. For example, a tool for knowledge elicitation might represent correlations among domain terms in a rating grid, while a tool for knowledge refinement might use a causal model to solve a problem and explain its solution.
- Inconsistent user roles—Each tool has different requirements. For example, a tool for systematic elicitation requires a user familiar with basic terminology and high-level rules. However, a tool for knowledge refinement requires a user capable of debugging complex problems with the knowledge base.
- Inconsistent user interface—Each tool presents the user with a different interface, which is an unnecessary source of confusion.

A final problem with the workbench approach concerns the specific tools that have been developed thus far. Many tools for acquiring the initial domain knowledge do not set the stage for the tools that follow them. Tools for knowledge refinement and knowledge reformulation require a support structure for domain knowledge. For example, Teiresias presents the inference path leading to an incorrect conclusion so that the domain expert can identify faulty inferences. However, many tools for systematic elicitation do not acquire the intermediate inferences that support conclusions. Because of such mismatches, many tools are inappropriate for the workbench.

Because of these problems with the workbench approach, our research pursues an alternative—a single tool that supports start-to-finish development of knowledge bases. Sections 3 and 4 describe our approach to solving two issues critical to the success of such a tool.

3. Protos: Continuous Support During Knowledge Acquisition

Protos is a knowledge-acquisition tool that supports knowledge elicitation and refinement. It learns to perform heuristic classification by solving problems under the guidance of an expert teacher. When the expert describes a case, Protos assigns the case to a known category and explains the classification. If the classification is wrong or the explanation is inadequate, Protos interacts with the expert to acquire knowledge. Its domain-independent method of classification suggests possible causes of problem-solving failures and guides interaction to extend and refine the knowledge base.

Protos' problem-solving ability and interaction with the expert improve as it acquires knowledge. Initially, Protos lacks adequate knowledge for problem solving. It fails to classify cases and depends on the expert to provide classifications and explanations. As Protos acquires more knowledge, it becomes increasingly able to perform classification. However, misclassifications are frequent, and its ability to discriminate is refined. Through this evolving interaction, Protos becomes an autonomous problem solver whose learning concentrates on acquiring specific knowledge to improve its ability to explain its classifications.

The following dialogue illustrates Protos' early interaction with the expert as it acquires knowledge to classify hearing disorders.

Expert: NewCase has the features: notch__at__4k, sensorineural:mild, hystory:noise, air:normal, speech:normal, static:normal, tympanogram:a, *et cetera*

Protos: These features suggest the classification normal__ear. To confirm this, a known case of normal__ear is being compared to NewCase. All features match except notch__at__4k, sensorineural:mild, and history:noise. Is normal__ear the collect classification?

Expert: No.

Protos: Are any of the unmatched features of NewCase incompatible with normal__ear?

Expert: All are.

Protos: Protos cannot classify NewCase. What is its classification?

Expert: Cochlear__noise.

Protos: Please explain the relevance of case features to this classification.

Expert: notch__at__4k is usually caused by cochlear__noise.
         et cetera

Protos: NewCase is being retained as the first exemplar of cochlear__noise.

Through this interaction, Protos refined its ability to discriminate instances of a known category of hearing disorder and acquired initial knowledge of a new one.

3.1. How Protos Performs Classification

Protos' classification method guides knowledge acquisition by relating steps in the classification process to the domain knowledge required to perform them successfully. Each type of failure suggests types of knowledge that are absent or faulty. This section describes the classification method and the knowledge it requires. Section 3.2 discusses how failures of the method guide knowledge acquisition.

Protos' method of classifying a case involves two steps. The first step is to hypothesize classifications based on the case's features (Figure 1). This step uses remindings, which are heuristic associations between features and categories learned from previous expert-provided explanations. The remindings associated with the features of a new case are combined to produce an ordered list of possible classifications.

The second step in classification attempts to confirm a hypothesis by matching the new case with prototypical exemplars (Figure 2). A process of *knowledge-based pattern matching* determines the similarity of the case and each exemplar. It uses previously acquired domain knowledge to explain how features of the case provide the same evidence as features of the exemplar. Overall similarity of the two cases is assessed by evaluating the quality of the resulting explanation and the importance of unmatched features.

If a match is imperfect, Protos searches for a more similar exemplar by traversing difference links associated with the current exemplar. Difference links connect exemplars and record their criterial differences.

Confirmation of the hypothesis is evaluated to determine Protos' next action. If the match is strong (i.e., adequately explained), it is presented to the user for approval and discussion. If it is weak, Protos considers other hypotheses and exemplars. Protos reports failure if its hypotheses are exhausted without finding an adequate match.[1]

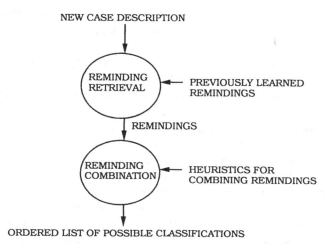

Figure 1. Step 1—Hypothesize classifications.

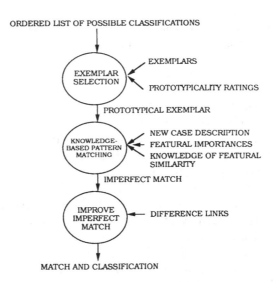

ORDERED LIST OF POSSIBLE CLASSIFICATIONS

EXEMPLAR SELECTION
— EXEMPLARS
— PROTOTYPICALITY RATINGS

PROTOTYPICAL EXEMPLAR

KNOWLEDGE-BASED PATTERN MATCHING
— NEW CASE DESCRIPTION
— FEATURAL IMPORTANCES
— KNOWLEDGE OF FEATURAL SIMILARITY

IMPERFECT MATCH

IMPROVE IMPERFECT MATCH
— DIFFERENCE LINKS

MATCH AND CLASSIFICATION

Figure 2. Step 2—Confirm a hypothesized classification.

3.2. How Failures Guide Knowledge Acquisition

Protos learns by analyzing and discussing failures of the classification method. The following general types of failures are possible:

1) Failure to classify—no classification can be determined
2) Failure to discriminate—an incorrect classification is reported
3) Failure to explain—the correct classification is inadequately explained

Protos associates each failure with a type of domain knowledge and interacts with the expert to acquire or refine the knowledge. Figure 3 presents Protos' algorithm for learning from failures.

Failure to classify a case indicates that Protos lacks knowledge of how a case's features determine its classification. The expert is asked to classify the case. Protos tries to relate each feature of the case to the provided classification by explaining its relevance. If Protos cannot relate a feature to the classification, the expert provides an explanation, which is added to the system's domain knowledge. After all of the features have been explained, the case is retained as a new exemplar of the classification.

Failure to discriminate occurs when Protos reports an incorrect classification. This indicates that Protos lacks knowledge to discriminate between instances and noninstances of the classification. Protos should not be able to match a new case to an exemplar of an incorrect classification. When such a match occurs, three possible causes are discussed with the expert. First, the expert is asked to evaluate the explanation relating the case and exemplar. Second, he is asked about unmatched features of the new case to determine whether any are incompatible with the classification. Third, he is asked for additional discriminating features.

```
GIVEN: a new case
FIND:  a classification of the case and an explanation of the
       classification

Search for an exemplar that matches the new case
IF not found
  THEN {classification failure}
       Ask teacher for classification
       Acquire explanations relating features to classification
       Compile remindings
       Retain case as an exemplar
  ELSE IF the teacher disapproves
          THEN {discrimination failure}
               Reassess remindings
               Discuss featural matches with the teacher
               Ask for discriminating features
               Remember unmatched features to add difference link
          ELSE {classification is correct}
               Increase exemplar's prototypicality rating
               IF match is incompletely explained
                  THEN {explanation failure}
                       Ask teacher for explanations of featural
                       equivalence
                       IF not given
                          THEN Retain case as exemplar
                          ELSE {processing was successful}
```

Figure 3. The Protos algorithm for learning from failures.

Failure to explain a correct classification indicates that Protos lacks knowledge to support its classification. Protos and the expert discuss improvements to the explanation of the match between the new case and the recalled exemplar. Unmatched features of the exemplar are of particular concern. For each, the expert is asked to identify a corresponding feature in the new case and to explain their relationship. If the expert cannot provide these explanations, the case is retained as a new exemplar.

Protos is also concerned with learning efficient problem solving. Just as it elicits and refines domain knowledge by discussing problem-solving failures, Protos acquires and refines an indexing structure of remindings, difference links, and prototypicality ratings. As discussed in Section 3.1, these indices limit the search for matching exemplars during classification.

When Protos fails to classify, it acquires remindings. To correct the failure, the expert provides explanations relating each case feature to the classification. Protos compiles the explanations into remindings that directly associate features and classifications. The strength of each reminding is determined by evaluating the explanation's quality, using heuristics similar to Cohen's path endorsements [Cohen and Kjeldsen, 1987; Bareiss, 1989].

When Protos fails to discriminate, it refines remindings. The remindings that suggested the incorrect classification are reassessed to determine whether they are consistent with the system's current knowledge. Because Protos is incrementally acquiring domain knowledge, it attempts to regenerate the explanation from which each reminding was compiled to determine whether it is still valid. If the explanation is no longer valid, the reminding is weakened or removed.

Protos also acquires a difference link when a failure to discriminate occurs. A difference link records important featural differences that distinguish two exemplars. Upon adding the new case as an exemplar, Protos creates a difference link between the case and the improperly matched exemplar. Protos suggests the features to annotate the difference link, and the expert approves them.

When a correct match occurs, Protos increases the exemplar's prototypicality rating. Prototypicality is determined by family resemblance, that is, the degree to which an exemplar matches other category members. An increased rating makes selection of the exemplar more likely during subsequent classification attempts.

Explanations play two roles in knowledge acquisition. First, explanations describe the relevance of exemplar features to categories. Such explanations enable remindings to be compiled and importance of features to classifications to be estimated. Second, explanations describe how different features provide equivalent evidence for a classification. Such explanations provide knowledge to match cases that are not uniformly described.

An explanation is a plausible chain of relations linking domain terms in the knowledge base (e.g., "fur is consistent with mammal which has specialization dog"). Explanations are expressed in a predefined language of relations (e.g., "causes," "co-occurs with," "has part"), qualifiers (e.g., "usually," "sometimes," "occasionally") and expert-supplied domain terms [Bareiss, 1989]. Heuristics associated with specific relations allow Protos to evaluate their plausibility in the context of a particular explanation [cf. Cohen and Kjeldsen, 1987].

In summary, Protos elicits and refines domain knowledge by interacting with the expert in the context of problem-solving failures. Through classification and discrimination failures, it acquires exemplars, an indexing structure, and general domain knowledge. Through explanation failures, it acquires the ability to explain its (otherwise correct) classifications.

3.3. An Example of Protos' Evolving Interaction

This section presents two examples illustrating how Protos' interaction with an expert audiologist evolved to support start-to-finish development of a knowledge base for classifying hearing disorders. The first example is from early in training; Protos systematically elicits knowledge of a new classification from the expert. The second example is from late in training; Protos refines its ability to explain an otherwise correct classification. To enable direct comparison of the two stages of training, *NewCase,* the case discussed in the introduction to Section 3, was presented to Protos twice. Independent copies of the knowledge base were used so that knowledge acquired by processing *NewCase* the first time did not affect its processing the second time.

3.3.1. Processing NewCase Early in Training
This example elaborates on the dialogue in the introduction to Section 3. *NewCase* was processed when Protos had seen few cases and lacked domain knowledge to classify correctly. At this stage of training, interaction with the expert primarily involved acquiring exemplars and systematically eliciting knowledge relating their features and classifications.

Based on past training, the features of *NewCase* (Figure 4) remind Protos of two possible diagnoses (Figure 5). When the individual remindings are combined, *normal_ear* is the strongest hypothesis. Protos retrieves the most prototypical exemplar of *normal_ear* and

Case: NewCase
Classification: Unknown

sensorineural: mild   i_acoustic_reflex: normal
notch_at_4k   c_acoustic_reflex: normal
history: noise   static: normal
speech: normal   tympanogram: a
oc_acoustic_reflex: normal   air: normal
oi_acoustic_reflex: elevated

Figure. 4. The features of the example case.

Case: NewCase
Classification: Unknown

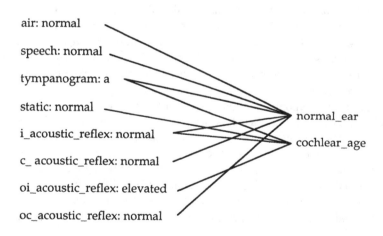

Figure. 5. Hypotheses associated with the features of *NewCase* when presented early in training.

attempts to match it to *NewCase* to confirm the hypothesis (Figure 6). Protos believes the match to be strong since all of the exemplar's features are matched. However, when the match is presented for discussion, the teacher rejects it as incorrect.

This failure to discriminate results in learning to classify cases of *normal__ear* more accurately. Since the exemplar's features are perfectly matched by *NewCase,* there are only a few possible reasons for the problem-solving failure. Protos pursues them systematically. First, Protos independently reassesses the remindings, which led it to *normal__ear,* with respect to its domain knowledge. It is able to regenerate the explanation from which each was compiled, suggesting that all are still valid. Second, Protos asks about the features of *NewCase* that were not matched by the exemplar and is told that all are incompatible

23

Case: NewCase   Case: p8447L

Classification: Unknown   Normal_Ear

air: normal ————————————— air: normal

speech: normal ————————————— speech: normal

tympanogram: a ————————— tympanogram: a

static: normal ————————————— static: normal

i_acoustic_reflex: normal ————————— i_acoustic_reflex: normal

c_ acoustic_reflex: normal ————————— c_ acoustic_reflex: normal

oi_acoustic_reflex: elevated ————————— oi_acoustic_reflex: elevated

oc_acoustic_reflex: normal ————————— oc_acoustic_reflex: normal

notch_at_4K

history: noise

sensorineural: mild

Figure. 6. Matching *NewCase* to an exemplar of normal ear.

with the classification. Third, when it asks whether the exemplar has additional features that discriminate it from *NewCase,* the teacher does not identify any.

Protos then tries to confirm its second diagnostic hypothesis, *cochlear__age.* It is unable to find an adequately similar exemplar of this category, so discussion with the teacher is not possible. Protos fails to confirm its hypothesis and, as before, reassesses the remindings that suggested *cochlear__age.*

Having exhausted the hypotheses, Protos reports a failure to classify. It asks the teacher to provide a classification, and he classifies *NewCase* as *cochlear__noise.* Since Protos has no exemplars of this category, *NewCase* is retained as an exemplar. Protos then interacts with the teacher to acquire general knowledge of *cochlear__noise.* It asks the teacher to explain the relevance of each case feature to the classification (using the predefined explanation language). The teacher provides explanations such as *"history:noise* is required by *cochlear__noise."* From these explanations, Protos compiles remindings linking the features and the classification. For example, *history: noise* is inferred to be highly predictive of *cochlear__noise.*

Since the failure to classify was preceded by a failure to discriminate, Protos installs a difference link between the new exemplar and the exemplar of *normal__ear* that is erroneously matched. The difference link is annotated with the features of *NewCase* that were not matched by features of the exemplar of *normal__ear.*

3.3.2. Processing NewCase Late in Training

After Protos had seen 175 cases, *NewCase* was presented to illustrate the shift from knowledge elicitation to refinement.[2] As it acquires knowledge, Protos becomes increasingly competent at problem solving and expects qualitatively different training from the expert. At this stage, Protos' classifications are generally correct, and interacton focuses on refining explanations.

As before, Protos hypothesizes classifications using remindings compiled from explanations of previous cases. Based on combining the remindings shown in Figure 7, Protos' best

Case: NewCase
Classification: Unknown

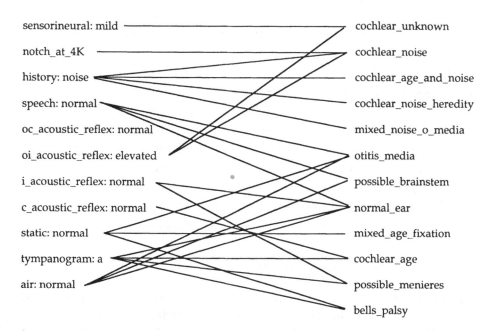

Figure. 7. Hypotheses associated with features of *NewCase* when presented late in training.

hypotheses are *cochlear__age&noise* and *cochlear__noise*. Protos rejects the first hypothesis when it cannot find a matching exemplar and reassesses the remindings to *cochlear__ age&noise*. It then tries *cochlear__noise* and finds a good match, which is illustrated in Figure 8.

Most of the features of the two cases match directly. The match between *sensorineural:mild* and *sensorineural:moderate* is an exception. Protos can match these features because of a past, expert-provided explanation that the two values of *sensorineural* are sometimes interchangeable in the context of this diagnosis.

Discussion with the expert focuses on Protos' failure to explain the match completely. Protos asks the expert whether the unmatched features of *NewCase* are equivalent to the unmatched exemplar features. He tells Protos:

> *notch__at__4k* is definitionally equivalent to *notch__4k*

and

> if the category is *cochlear__noise* then *c__acoustic__reflex: normal*
> is sometimes interchangeable with *c__acoustic__reflex: elevated*

Protos does not retain *NewCase* because any future case that would match *NewCase* would match the existing exemplar equally well. The prototypicality of the exemplar is increased to credit its participation in a close, successful match.

Case: NewCase   Case: p8572R

Classification: Unknown   Cochlear_noise

NewCase	Cochlear_noise
sensorineural: mild ———————————	sensorineural: moderate
notch_at_4k	notch_4k
history: noise ———————————	history: noise
speech: normal ———————————	speech: normal
oc_acoustic_reflex: normal —————	oc_acoustic_reflex: normal
oi_acoustic_reflex: elevated ————	oi_acoustic_reflex: elevated
i_acoustic_reflex: normal —————	i_acoustic_reflex: normal
c_acoustic_reflex: normal	c_acoustic_reflex: elevated
static: normal ———————————	static: normal
tympanogram: a ———————————	tympanogram: a
air: normal ———————————	air: normal

Figure 8. Matching *NewCase* to an exemplar of cochlear__noise.

Processing *NewCase* at two points in the evolution of the audiology knowledge base illustrates how Protos supports different stages of knowledge acquisition. The first time *NewCase* was processed, the system had little domain knowledge and was unable to classify it correctly. Through discussing the failure to classify, Protos acquired knowledge of a new classification, an exemplar, and the relevance of the exemplar's features to the classification. The expert was asked to provide a considerable amount of explanation relating *NewCase* to the system's existing knowledge. Discussion of the failure to discriminate *NewCase* from a case of *normal__ear* refined Protos' indexing knowledge.

The second time *NewCase* was processed, Protos had more extensive knowledge and could determine the correct classification independently. The expert played the more limited role of explaining relationships between features, which improved Protos' ability to explain its classification.

3.4. Evaluating Protos in Clinical Audiology

A distinct advantage of studying knowledge acquisition for expert systems is the evaluation criteria that it affords. Problem-solving proficiency can be measured as knowledge accumulates and, ultimately, can be compared with human experts. It is somewhat surprising that, with few exceptions [*e.g.*, Quinlin, 1986; Michalski, 1987], knowledge acquisition tools have not been evaluated. This section describes some of the data collected to assess Protos' viability.

Protos was trained using 200 hearing-disorder cases from the files of a large clinic. The training set was random. Its size was restricted to 200 cases because this is approximately the number of cases that a human audiologist sees during graduate school. For Protos to be considered successful, it was deemed necessary for the system to classify accurately and efficiently given a similar amount of training. After training, Protos' performance was evaluated using a random set of 26 new cases. The characteristics of the training and test cases are presented in Table 1.

The fundamental assessment of Protos' performance is the correctness of its classifications. Protos correctly classified 82% of the training set while learning. Afterwards, Protos correctly classified 100% of the test cases.[3]

Table 1. Characteristics of Cases Presented to Protos

Characteristic	Training Set	Test Set
Number of Cases	200	26
Number of Categories	24	6
Exemplars Retained	120	—
Mean Features/Case	10.6	11.5
(Total number of features=73)		

Protos' problem-solving efficiency can be measured by the amount of effort it expended during classification. The average number of diagnostic hypotheses pursued and the number of matches attempted gradually increased (Table 2). However, as a percentage of possible hypotheses, the number of hypotheses pursued decreased. As a percentage of possible exemplars, the number of matches attempted remained fairly constant. The number of matches presented to the expert remained fairly constant as well. The corresponding percentage decreased, indicating increasing autonomy. Most of the classification process was independent of the expert.

Table 2. Classification Effort Expended

Cases	Hypotheses Pursued	Matches Attempted	Matches Discussed
1–50	2.7 (25.5%)	not available	1.7 (3.7%)
51–100	2.8 (17.5%)	not available	1.6 (1.9%)
101–150	2.5 (11.9%)	4.6 (4.4%)	1.5 (1.4%)
151–200	4.0 (16.7%)	7.4 (6.2%)	1.9 (1.6%)
average	3.0	6.0	1.6
test	3.7 (15.4%)	5.3 (4.4%)	1.1 (0.9%)

The evolution of Protos' interaction with the expert can be seen in a gradual shift in the type of explanations Protos elicited (Figure 9). As the knowledge base evolved, Protos' focus shifted from attaining competence at classification to attaining competence at explanation. Early training was dominated by classification failures. Protos primarily elicited explanations relating features to classifications as new exemplars were retained. Gradually, classification failures were superceded by explanation failures, and interaction with the teacher shifted to explaining the similarity of features in the context of particular diagnostic categories. This knowledge refined the system's ability to explain its correct classifications.

The design of Protos and its experimental evaluation in the domain of clinical audiology are more completely described in Bareiss [1989]. A Common Lisp implementation of Protos is available [Dvorak, 1988] and has been widely distributed.

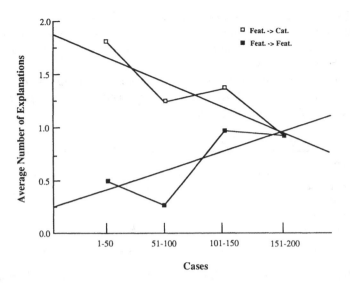

Figure 9. Teacher-provided explanations per case.

3.5. Strengths and Limitations

Protos' primary strength as a knowledge-acquisition tool is its knowledge of the classification method. This initial knowledge relates steps in the classification process to the domain knowledge required to perform them. In particular, Protos relates failures during classification to particular forms of knowledge that are absent or faulty. This rich decomposition of the problem-solving task is perhaps the most useful form of a priori knowledge for knowledge-acquisition tools. [Bylander and Chandrasekaran, 1987].

Protos' classification method is effective during both systematic elicitation and knowledge refinement. Initially, Protos is unable to classify cases, and it acquires knowledge from the expert in the form of explained examples. As Protos acquires more knowledge, it becomes increasingly able to classify cases, although misclassifications are common. Using explicit knowledge of possible failures, Protos interacts with the expert to refine the knowledge base. Protos becomes an autonomous problem solver and acquires knowledge to improve its ability to explain its classifications. However, Protos' classification method is ineffective for determining the consequences of knowledge-base modifications and extensions. As with most knowledge-acquisition tools, Protos is a "lazy evaluator" of new information. Some of the consequences of a knowledge-base change are revealed during problem solving, which is interleaved with knowledge acquisition; other consequences are undetected. "Eager evaluation" of new information is preferred for two reasons. First, it detects inconsistencies and knowledge-base gaps before they cause failures. Second, it enables a tool to respond to new information with follow-up inferences and questions. The next section describes a tool that performs this task and identifies the required knowledge.

4. KI: Integrating New Information During Knowledge Refinement

KI is a knowledge acquisition tool being developed to support integrating new information during knowledge refinement. Although this research is preliminary, a prototype of KI has been implemented that demonstrates several benefits from aggressively evaluating knowledge-base modifications and extensions. When new information is provided, KI uses the existing knowledge to critique the new information and determine its consequences. Determining these consequences reveals inconsistencies and gaps in the knowledge base. KI elicits information from the knowledge engineer to fill the gaps and resolve the inconsistencies. KI's computational model of knowledge integration includes three prominent activities:

1) Recognition—identifying the knowledge relevant to new information
2) Elaboration—applying the expectations provided by relevant knowledge to determine the consequences of the new information
3) Adaptation—modifying the knowledge base to accommodate the elaborated information

Current knowledge refinement tools avoid in-depth evaluation of knowledge acquired during knowledge refinement. Some tools simply add new information and ignore its consequences, assuming that inconsistencies will be exposed as problem-solving failures and corrected as they occur. Other approaches have been limited to detecting surface inconsistencies [e.g., Davis, 1977; Wilkins, 1988]; however, these approaches cannot detect subtle inconsistencies introduced by knowledge-base revisions, because they ignore implicit consequences of new information for existing domain knowledge. FIE [Cohen, 1984] improves on these approaches by using resolution to determine the shallow interaction between new information and existing beliefs. However, this approach lacks sufficient control to integrate extensions into a large knowledge base or to identify the deep consequences of new information.

KI's approach to controllng the search for the consequences of new information uses a form of domain knowledge called *views*. Each view defines a segment of the knowledge base comprised of concepts that interact in some significant way. Views are used to heuristically guide the search during knowledge integration by identifying the inference paths worth pursuing when the representation of a concept is extended with new information.

KI is being developed to assist knowledge engineers to extend the Botany Knowledge Base [Porter, Lester, Murray, Pittman, Souther, Acker, and Jones, 1988], which contains approximately 4,000 frames representing task-independent knowledge about plant anatomy, physiology, and development. The following sections describe KI's preliminary development. Section 4.1 describes an example of knowledge integration that is representative of the complex knowledge-base extensions we expect KI to perform. A prototype implementation of KI has been successfully tested with this example. Sections 4.2 through 4.4 describe how KI performs the tasks of recognition, elaboration, and adaptation. In Section 4.5, the strengths and limitations of this approach are reviewed.

4.1. An Example of Knowledge Integration

This example involves extending the knowledge base with new information about plant seeds. The knowledge base already has the information that plant seeds contain nutritive tissue called endosperm (which is analogous to an egg's yoke). The plant embryo consumes the endosperm during its development inside the seed. A knowledge engineer wishes to extend the knowledge base with a representation of *nonendospermic seed,* a type of seed that contains no endosperm. The task of KI is to interact with the knowledge engineer to integrate this new information. The knowledge engineer presents new information to KI:[4]

Knowledge Engineer: There is a class of seeds that have no endosperm.

With assistance from the knowledge engineer, KI identifies and retrieves knowledge structures relevant to this new information. Using inference rules defined for the retrieved knowledge structures, KI forms the expectation that the embryo in a nonendospermic seed will die of starvation. It then attempts to confirm this expectation with the knowledge engineer:

KI: Endosperm is a source of plant nutrients; is this relevant?
Knowledge Engineer: Yes.
KI: Seeds without endosperm do not give rise to healthy seedlings.
Knowledge Engineer: Explain.
KI: The embryo starves since the endosperm provides nutrients, and nutrients are essential for health and survival.
Knowledge Engineer: Yes, nutrients are essential; however, the embryo survives.

KI attempts to resolve the inconsistency between its expectations and the assertion that embryos in nonendospermic seeds survive. One possible explanation is that these embryos acquire nutrients from some other source. KI searches for alternate ways an embryo-stage plant might acquire nutrients. A focused discussion with the knowledge engineer ensues that resolves the anomaly and extends the knowledge base.

KI: Does the embryo acquire nutrients from photosynthesis?
Knowledge Engineer: Yes, the shoots of some plant embryos emerge from the seed during germination and start producing photosynthate.

As this example illustrates, KI integrates new information by determining its consequences. When conflicts are encountered, KI searches for alternative explanations to resolve them. The computational issues that arise during knowledge integration include identifying knowledge relevant to new information, relating relevant knowledge to the new information, and adapting the knowledge base to accommodate the new information. The following three sections describe in greater detail how KI performs these activities.

4.2. Recognition

KI begins knowledge integration by identifying relevant knowledge structures. In the previous example about seeds with no endosperm, KI must determine which among the thousands of frames in the Botany Knowledge Base may be affected in some way.

The representation of each object in the Botany Knowledge Base is structured with views to focus the search for knowledge relevant to new information. Each view is a segment of the knowledge base that identifies concepts that interact in some significant way. Perspectives are a common type of view that represent concepts in particular roles. For example, one perspective of endosperm is *Plant Food Source,* as shown in Figure 10. Other perspectives include: endosperm as a *Product Of Reproduction*, endosperm as a *Contained Object*, and endosperm as a *Taxon Defining Part*. KI collects the views for objects referenced by new information and prompts the knowledge engineer to select which are appropriate.

A view is represented as a semantic-net template that can be instantiated for hypothetical objects. KI instantiates the views selected by the knowledge engineer. The instantiation of *Plant Food Source* for an endosperm is presented in Figure 11. Collectively, these instantiated frames comprise a *context* representing an endosperm in its role as a plant food source; this context is used to simulate the effects of the new information about endosperm.

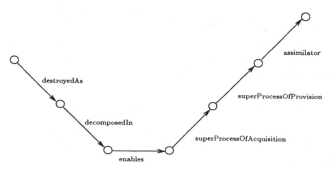

This perspective, represented as a semantic-net template, defines the concepts relevant to an object in its role as a plant food source: a plant food source must have a stage when it is destroyed and decomposed into nutrients; this decomposition enables the nutrients to be assimilated by the plant; nutrient assimilation involves the provision and acquisition of nutrients.

Figure 10. The perspective *Plant Food Source.*

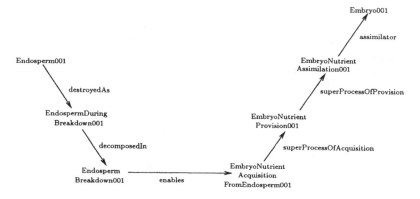

The perspective of Figure 10 is instantiated for a hypothetical endosperm: the endosperm is decomposed into nutrients which are assimilated by a hypothetical plant embryo. This context is used to simulate the effects of seeds not having endosperms.

Figure 11. The context created by instantiating *Plant Food Source.*

31

4.3. Elaboration

During recognition, KI creates a context by instantiating concepts in the knowledge base most relevant to the new information. Next, during elaboration, KI determines how the new information interacts with existing knowledge within this context. Elaboration involves applying inference rules to propagate the effects of the new information throughout the context.

In the endosperm example, elaboration begins when KI asserts that the endosperm is absent from the context by assigning value *False* to the slot *enabled?* of *Endosperm 001*. This assignment triggers inference rules that determine the consequences of seeds lacking endosperm. For example, without the endosperm, the embryo cannot get enough nutrients to survive. Only rules that apply to frames in the context are considered; therefore, by selectively instantiating frames during recognition, KI controls the inferences that are attempted during elaboration. The inference rules applicable to this example are listed in Figure 12, and the elaborated context is presented in Figure 13.

1. When an entity is disabled, all of its developmental stages are disabled.
2. When an entity is disabled, all the processes involving the entity are disabled.
3. When a process is disabled, all the processes that its completion enables are disabled.
4. When the known methods of acquiring some essential resource are disabled, the rate of providing the resource is inadequate for survival.
5. When the assimilation rate for some resource is unknown, it is the same as the provision rate.
6. When nutrient assimilation is inadequate for survival, the assimilator is dying.

Figure 12. Heuristic rules relevant to endosperm as a plant food source.

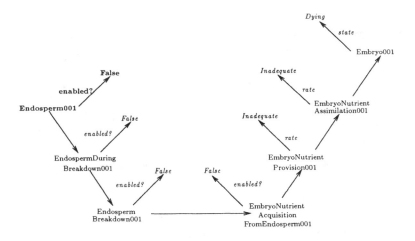

The hypothetical endosperm is disabled, triggering the inference rules of Figure 12, which propagate the effects of this assertion throughout the context. The predicted consequences of seeds lacking endosperms are presented in italics.

Figure 13. The elaborated context.

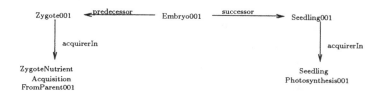

The context of Figure 13 is extended to include the developmental predecessor and successor of *Embryo 001* and their methods of nutrient acquisition.

Figure 14. The context extension.

Through elaboration, KI concludes that the plant embryo is dying from lack of nutrients. This triggers the instantiatin of a second view defined for plants that are starving and in danger of dying. The original context is expanded to include the plant's developmental stages immediately before and after its embryo stage and how nutrients are acquired during each of these developmental stages. This additional knowledge is presented in Figure 14. Through continued elaboration, KI concludes that the plant's seedling stage is not reached because the plant dies during its embryo stage.

An important function of elaboration is identifying confounded expectations. These occur when expectations of the knowledge base are violated by new information or when two rules reach conflicting conclusions. Resolving inconsistencies involves correcting the new information to comply with current expectations or adapting the existing knowledge structures to accommodate the new information.

4.4. Adaptation

Elaboration reveals anomalies in the knowledge base; adaptation resolves them. An anomaly can result from inconsistencies introduced either by inference rules used during elaboration or by facts the knowledge engineer asserts. In the endosperm example, an anomaly is detected when the knowledge engineer asserts that the embryos of nonendospermic seeds survive, correcting the prediction that these embryos starve.

Resolving anomalies requires correcting explanations that support failed expectations and constructing alternative explanations to account for new information. When the knowledge engineer refutes the prediction that embryos of nonendospermic seeds starve, KI inspects the explanation for this prediction to determine its weakest premise. This suspect explanation is presented in Figure 15. Rule 4 (from Figure 12) relies on a closed-world assumption and is considered a relatively weak inference. Therefore, KI retracts its conclusion and assumes *Embryo Nutrient Provision 001* is adequate for the embryo's survival. This change propagates through the explanation, retracting the belief that the embryo starves.

The original anomaly has been resolved by assuming that the embryos of nonendospermic seeds receive adequate nutrients. However, no alternative method is known for plant embryos to acquire nutrients. KI seeks to construct an explanation for the assumed nutrient acquisition using the following inference:

If a resource provision is adequate for survival, but no acquisition method is known, then assume the acquisition method of the developmental successor is employed.

Figure 15. The suspect explanation.

This rule suggests the embryos of nonendospermic seeds acquire nutrients by photosynthesis, as is done by seedlings. However, this hypothesis introduces new constraints on the embryos of nonendospermic seeds. For example, to acquire nutrients by photosynthesis, the embryo must be a photosynthetic plant. Therefore, to apply this inference, KI asserts that *Embryo 001* is an instance of *Photosynthetic Plant*. As a photosynthetic plant, the embryo inherits the following features: it contacts sunlight, and its composition includes chlorophyll. This is illustrated in Figure 16. In short, the plausibility of explaining the survival of nonendospermic embryos by assuming they engage in photosynthesis is contingent on their contacting sunlight and possessing chlorophyll. Confirming these assumptions leads to the acquisition of further knowledge from the knowledge engineer.

4.5. KI's Strengths and Limitations

KI can partially determine the consequences of new information because it has access to substantial domain expertise and a method for heuristically determining what existing knowledge is relevant. Using existing knowledge to elaborate new information enables KI to acquire more than what is literally expressed by the new information. KI uncovers implicit conflicts between new information and existing knowledge and assists the knowledge engineer with resolving them. However, because our approach assumes substantial domain knowledge, it is inappropriate during the initial stages of knowledge-base development when the encoded domain expertise is sparse.

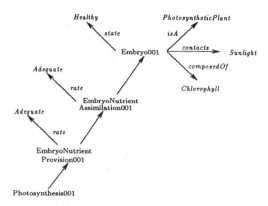

The context is adapted to account for adequate nutrient provision when no nutrients are acquired from the endosperm. Assuming the plant embryo acquires nutrients through photosynthesis requires that it contacts sunlight and possesses chlorophyll.

Figure 16. The adapted context.

Identifying all interactions between new information and existing knowledge is intractable; performing knowledge integration requires restricting this search. KI uses views in two ways to avoid an intractable search. First, views are used as a control mechanism to provide a coarse granularity in searching for the consequences of new information. This permits KI to efficiently identify deep consequences of new information within selected contexts. Second, views define local, computational environments. We are developing KI to enforce consistency of the knowledge-base within views. This policy operationalizes the adage of maintaining *local consistency* and obviates the intractable task of computing the deductive closure of the knowledge base.

Our prototype implementation of KI has two shortcomings, which our current research partially addresses. First, the knowledge engineer is required to choose from views that KI considers relevant. We are designing an agenda-based search mechanism that automates view selection [Murray and Porter, 1989]. Second, views are rigid because each is represented by an explicit path of slots (as in Figure 10). The number of views needed to structure a knowledge base is large, and each view is manually created. We are studying alternative representations of views [e.g., Porter, Souther, Lester, and Acker, 1989] and ways to acquire views during knowledge integration.

5. Summary

Knowledge-acquisition tools help with knowledge-base development—the progression of a knowledge base from a level of complete ignorance to a desired level of knowledge. Development typically involves three stages: elicitation of initial knowledge, refinement of a prototype knowledge base, and reformulation of knowledge to improve performance. Each stage requires a particular form of assistance, and most knowledge-acquisition tools support only a single stage.

Conceivably, start-to-finish development of knowledge bases could be supported by a workbench of tools. The workbench organizes a collection of tools, each of which helps with a particular development stage. However, the support is not continuous, and many current tools are inappropriate for the workbench because they do not acquire the knowledge that subsequent tools require.

Our research pursues an alternative—supporting start-to-finish development of knowledge bases with a single tool. We have studied two issues crucial to building such a tool. The first issue is spanning multiple stages of development. We have built Protos, a tool that acquires knowledge while assisting a domain expert to solve classification problems. Initially, Protos' knowledge is inadequate for solving problems; it interviews the expert to acquire the domain's conceptual structure. As the knowledge base develops, problem solving improves and errors are discussed with the expert to refine the knowledge base. Protos becomes an autonomous problem solver and continues to improve its ability to explain its classifications. Its effectiveness has been demonstrated with the construction of a knowledge-based system for diagnosing hearing disorders.

The second issue addressed by our research is knowledge integration. As a large-scale knowledge base is developed, the importance and the difficulty of performing knowledge integration increases. We are building KI, a tool that evaluates new information to determine its consequences for existing knowledge. KI controls the search for consequences with a form of domain knowledge called views. Each view identifies the inference paths to pursue when the representation of a concept is extended with new information. We are applying KI to make complex extensions to a large-scale knowledge base.

Acknowledgments

Support for this research was provided by the Army Research Office under grant ARO-DAAG29-84-K-0060, the National Science Foundation under grant IRI-8620052, and contributions by Apple, Texas Instruments, and the Cray Foundation. We are indebted to Professor Craig Wier for serving as the domain expert for the application of Protos to clinical audiology and to Professor James Jerger of the Baylor College of Medicine for providing the training cases. We are grateful to Robert Holte for providing useful commentary on early drafts of this report. We appreciate the assistance of Joe Ross, Claudia Porter, and Ken Murray during the development of Protos. Ken Murray and Bruce Porter are the primary researchers on the KI project, with substantial contributions from Art Souther, Liane Acker, James Lester, and Karen Pittman.

Notes

1. Protos does not consider all of the categories of which it is reminded. Only the strongest remindings are considered. Furthermore a category is considered only if no matching subordinate category can be found.
2. Again, an independent copy of the knowledge base was used that did not contain *NewCase* or the associated indices and domain knowledge.

3. Note that the ability to classify cases into *known* categories is being reported; the 24 training instances that introduced new diagnostic categories are excluded from the training percentage.
4. This example has been simplified for presentation. For example, KI does not generate and parse natural language; this discourse has been converted from a language of frames, slots, and values. A complete description of the prototype implementation and this example are provided in Murray [1988].

References

Bareiss, R. 1989. *Exemplar-based knowledge acquisition: A unified approach to concept representation, classification, and learning.* (Based on PhD dissertation, University of Texas at Austin, Austin, TX: Department of Computer Sciences), Academic Press.

Bennett, J.S. 1985. ROGET: A knowledge-based system for acquiring the conceptual structure of a diagnostic expert system. *Automated Reasoning, 1,* 49-74.

Boose, J. 1984. Personal construct theory and the transfer of expertise. *Proceedings of the National Conference on Artificial Intelligence,* (pp. 27-33).

Boose, J., and Bradshaw, J. 1987. Expertise transfer and complex problems: Using Aquinus as a knowledge acquisition workbench for knowledge-based systems. *International Journal of Man-Machine Studies 26,* 1, 3-28.

Bylander, T., and Chandrasekaran, B. 1987. Generic tasks for knowledge-based reasoning: The right level of abstraction for knowledge acquisition. *International Journal of Man-Machine Studies 26,* 231-243.

Clancey, W.J. 1985. Heuristic classification. *Artificial Intelligence 27,* 289-350.

Cohen, P., and Kjeldsen, R. 1987. Information retrieval by constrained spreading activation in semantic networks. *Information Processing and Management 23,* 255-268.

Davis, R. 1977. Interactive transfer of expertise: Acquisition of new inference rules. *Proceedings of the International Joint Conference on Artificial Intelligence* (pp. 321-328).

Dvorak, D. 1988. *Guide to CL-Protos: An exemplar-based learning apprentice.* (Technical Report AI88-87). Austin, TX: University of Texas, Department of Computer Sciences.

Eshelman, L., Ehret, D., McDermott, J., and Tan, M. 1987. MOLE: A tenacious knowledge acquisition tool. *International Journal of Man-Machine Studies 26,* 41-54.

Kahn, G., Nowlan, S., and McDermott, J. 1985. MORE: An intelligence knowledge acquisition tool. *Proceedings of the International Joint Conference on Artificial Intelligence* (pp. 581-584).

Michalski, R.S. 1987. How to learn imprecise concepts: a method for employing a two-tiered knowledge representation in learning. *Proceedings of the Fourth International Workshop on Machine Learning* (pp. 50-58).

Mitchell, T.M., Mahadevan, S., and Steinberg, L.I. 1985. LEAP: A learning apprentice for VLSI design. *Proceedings of the International Joint Conference on Artificial Intelligence* (pp. 573-580).

Murray, K. 1988. *KI: An Experiment in Automating Knowledge Integration.* (Technical Report AI88-90). Austin, TX: University of Texas, Department of Computer Sciences.

Murray, K., and Porter, B. 1989. Controlling search for the consequences of new information during knowledge integration. *Proceedings of the Sixth International Workshop on Machine Learning* (pp. 290-295).

Musen, M.A., Fagan, L.M., Combs, D.M., and Shortliffe, E.H. 1987. Use of a domain model to drive an interactive knowledge-editing tool. *International Journal of Man-Machine Studies 26,* 105-121.

Neches, R., Swartout, W.R., and Moore, J.D. 1985. Enhanced maintenance and explanation of expert systems through explicit models of their development. *IEEE Transactions on Software Engineering 11,* 1337-1351.

Porter, B., Souther, A., Lester, J., and Acker, L. 1989. Generating explanations in an intelligent tutor designed to teach fundamental knowledge. *Proceedings of the 2nd Intelligent Tutoring Systems Research Forum,* (pp. 55-69).

Quinlan, J.R. 1986 Induction of Decision Trees. *Machine Learning 1,* 81-106.

Smith, R.G., Winston, H.A., Mitchell, T.M., and Buchanan, B.G. 1985. Representation and use of explicit justifications for knowledge base refinements. *Proceedings of the Ninth International Joint Conference on Artificial Intelligence* (pp. 673-680).

Wilkins, D.C. 1988. Knowledge base refinement using apprenticeship learning techniques. *Proceedings of the National Conference on Artificial Intelligence* (pp. 646-651).

Machine Learning, 4, 285–291 (1989)

The Knowledge Level Reinterpreted: Modeling How Systems Interact

WILLIAM J. CLANCEY
Institute for Research on Learning, 2550 Hanover Street, Palo Alto, CA 94304

Machine learning will never progress beyond its current state until people realize that knowledge is not a substance that can be stored. Knowledge acquisition, in particular, is a process of developing computer models, often for the first time, not a process of transferring or accessing statements or diagrams that are already written down and filed away in an expert's mind. The "knowledge acquisition bottleneck" is a wrong and misleading metaphor, suggesting that the problem is to squeeze a large amount of already-formed concepts and relations through a narrow communication channel; the metaphor seriously misconstrues the theory formation process of computer modeling. The difficulties of choosing and evaluating knowledge acquisition methods are founded on a number of related misconceptions, clarified as follows: 1) the primary concern of knowledge engineering is modeling systems in the world (not replicating how people think—a matter for psychology); 2) knowledge-level analysis is how observers describe and explain the recurrent behaviors of a situated system, that is, some system interacting with an embedding environment; the knowledge level describes the *product* of an evolving, adaptive interaction between the situated system and its environment, not the internal, physical processes of an isolated system; 3) modeling intelligent behavior is fraught with frame-of-reference confusions, requiring that we tease apart the roles and points of view of the human expert, the mechanical devices he interacts with, the social and physical environment, and the observer-theoretician (with his own interacting suite of recording devices, representations, and purposes). The challenge to knowledge acquisition today is to clarify what we are doing (computer modeling), clarify the difficult problems (the nature of knowledge and representations), and reformulate our research program accordingly.

1. Qualitative Process Modeling

In the past decade, we have studied knowledge bases and abstracted their designs, so we can describe what we are doing and devise methods to do it more clearly, reliably, and efficiently. Second generation expert systems separate out and make explicit the two processes that are modeled in every expert system: a model of some system in the world (the domain, e.g., a model of an electronic circuit) and a model of reasoning processes (the inference procedure, e.g., a diagnostic procedure) [Clancey 1983]. These two aspects of expert systems are reflected in two dominant, interacting areas of research, called *qualitative reasoning* and *generic systems*, respectively. The focus of qualitative reasoning is to develop notations and calculi for modeling processes in the world. The focus of generic systems is to develop task-specific representations and inference procedures (e.g., specific to diagnosis, configuration, scheduling, auditing, and control) [Clancey 1985]. These complementary areas of research are integrated in expert systems and associated tools with enhanced capability for knowledge acquisition and explanation. Second generation expert system techniques provide a growing library of abstractions, enabling new programs to be constructed by reusing and refining existing representations and inference procedures. The papers in this special issue make contributions to this research.

Progress to date has followed from the realization that improved expert system explanation, knowledge acquisition, and maintenance depend on abstracted descriptions of the content of knowledge bases and, only secondarily, on the development of alternative representational notations. We call this content analysis "knowledge-level analysis," and contrast it with earlier emphasis on implementation-level concerns (e.g., using rules versus frames). The earlier questions about notations do not go away, but rather are recast in categorical analysis of the nature of the task and system being modeled (e.g., an isolated, designed device versus a biological, open system), how processes are modeled (e.g., classification versus simulation), the inference method for constructing a situation-specific model (e.g., contrasting alternatives on a blackboard versus depth-first, incremental refinement), and the macro structure of the relational network used for describing the domain and inferential processes (i.e., hierarchies, state-transition networks, and compositions of these) [Clancey 1989]. Questions of computer encoding are thus reformulated in terms of process modeling methods that emphasize decomposition and layering of representations.

In short, the first step in clarifying the nature of knowledge engineering is realizing that all knowledge bases contain models of systems in the world and that the expert serves as informant about how such systems tend to behave, how they can be designed or controlled to generate desirable behaviors, and how they can be assembled or repaired. An immediate, important consequence of this realization is that an expert system's performance can be evaluated in terms of the suitability of the model it constructs for the purpose at hand. For example, for medical diagnosis we need to look beyond the name of the diseases output by the program to determine whether the preferred diagnosis covers the symptoms that require explanation [Clancey 1986]. Previously, such consideration of completeness and consistency was reserved for programs using simulation or so-called model-based reasoning. Now we realize that all expert systems are carrying out a modeling task and can be evaluated on this basis.

To spell this out more explicitly, we now realize that qualitative reasoning embraces modeling based on classifications (e.g., a taxonomy of disease processes), as well as modeling based on simulations (e.g., a behavioral simulation in the form of a causal network relating abnormal substances and processes internal to the system being modeled). For this reason, from the second generation viewpoint, we define knowledge engineering as a *methodology for modeling processes qualitatively*, in the form of relational networks describing causal, temporal, and spatial relations. Naturally, it is useful to integrate qualitative with numeric models, and we are belatedly discovering that many expert systems have done this all along (e.g., SOPHIE used qualitative modeling to control and interpret a FORTRAN simulation of its electronic circuit [Brown, et al. 1982]; SACON used simplified numeric equations to estimate stress and deflection, which were then abstracted to select programs that provide more detailed analysis [Bennett, et al. 1978]).

The knowledge engineering community's disparagement of classification goes beyond the suggestion that it is not modeling. Many papers in the literature suggest that classification models are inferior to simulation models and can be entirely reduced to or compiled from them. According to this point of view, physicians talk in terms of syndromes and disease classifications because they do not understand the causal mechanisms causing these processes. A "real" model would reduce disease descriptions to descriptions of physical structure and function. For the most part, this belief is false and belies a fundamental misunderstanding about the nature of system modeling and, more generally, how systems interact.

Disease descriptions characterize *the result of recurrent interaction* between an individual person and his environment. Consider for example tennis elbow. This syndrome cannot be causally explained in terms of processes lying exclusively within the person or within the environment. Rather it is a result of a pattern of interaction between the person and environment over time. As for any emergent effect, it cannot be predicted, explained, or controlled by treating the person in isolation or even by studying the person-environment system over short periods. It is a developmental effect, an adaptation in the person that reflects the history of his behavior. The same claim can be made about the entire taxonomy of medical diseases—trauma, toxicity, infection, neoplasms, and congenital disorders—they are all descriptions of bodily processes after a history of recurrent interactions. Similar examples can be drawn from computer system failures; faults cannot be reduced to changes in a blueprint, but are in fact constantly introduced and prone to change in an open environment. A favorite story at Stanford's SUMEX-AIM is how system crashes were caused every fall when the first October rains wet the phone lines going to Santa Cruz, swamping the computer with spurious control-Cs attempting to get its attention. Such problems aren't fixed by swapping boards.

The consequences of this systems modeling perspective are more staggering than you might first imagine. We are led to realize that beyond the blueprints and functional diagrams of a device being modeled (including the human body), if the device is situated, that is, interacting with an open environment, then a classification model is necessary in order to characterize how the device will appear after it has adapted to a history of interactions with its environment. Such descriptions are necessary in order to describe the state of the device, to explain—historically—how it got into this state, and thus to provide a basis for modifying or controlling the system in some desired way (e.g., to prevent the tennis elbow from recurring). Such descriptions are relative to an observer's point of view; they are not to be confused with the internal mechanisms in the device that produce its moment-by-moment behaviors. To put it simply, a category jump has been made: The system we are now describing is the environment and the embedded device interacting over time, not the device in isolation. Thus, classification models constitute a level of system description, but they cannot be reduced to or mapped onto physical structures in individual devices. As we move from blueprint-like structure–function models, we move from the domain of an isolated system to social, interactive, emergent processes. As Ryle warned us, we make a category mistake if we try to find the university in the members of colleges, the division in the parade of soldier battalions, or team spirit in specific "cricketing operations" [Ryle 1949]. It is no coincidence that Ryle's examples all contrast social organizations with individuals or aspects viewed in isolation. To suppose that classification models can be reduced to the mechanisms of individual agents is to make a category mistake.

At this point it becomes clear that we have to be much more careful in modeling situated systems. We are interested not only in how a device works internally, but how its behavior develops in different interactional environments. This is precisely the province of the human expert, who can tell us what he has observed from experience, as he has participated in the device's operation. For different purposes, we may find it necessary to get the viewpoint of different observers, yielding not one true model of reality, but descriptions relative to different points of view. A great deal can be said about frame of reference problems as a way of synthesizing recent work on situated automata and situated cognition (see [Clancey, in preparation]).

2. Knowledge and Representations

From here it is a simple step to realize that knowledge-level descriptions of human behavior are also descriptions and explanations that an observer gives of a situated system. Knowledge is something an observer ascribes to a human agent in order to describe and explain recurrent interactions the agent has with his environment. Knowledge-level descriptions cannot be reduced to mechanisms in the body of individual agents; they are relative to the observer's point of view and characterize the total system of agent plus environment. Furthermore (now taking a much bolder leap), a knowledge-level description, as a representation, must be expressed in some perceived medium; representations are not stored as or translated from internal structures. For example, when we speak, we are not translating internal representations of what our words mean. Representations only exist physically in an observer's statements, drawings, computer programs, silent speech, visualizations, etc.; otherwise, no observation has occurred. Representations of knowledge are always open to interpretation; their meaning is never fixed or defined, but always relative to an observer's frame of reference. Thus, a secondary level of relativity is interposed by the observer of the observer's representations.

To go back a few steps and summarize, we find ourselves almost overwhelmed with reasons for believing that a knowledge base cannot be associated with structures that were already encoded in the head of the expert:

- Knowledge-level descriptions are attributions made by an observer (the knowledge engineer), involving his own selective interactions with the agent (the expert), his own perceptions, and his point of view;
- Knowledge-level descriptions abstract a sequence of behaviors (what the expert does and says in the course of solving a sequence of problem examples), not single, moment-by-moment responses;
- Descriptions of the device being modeled and inferential processes are informed by the expert's observations and problem-solving behavior, but they are not primarily intended to be the expert's "mental models" or psychological explanations of his behavior.
- To the extent that the processes people follow in gathering data to solve a problem and taking action in the world are intended to be simulated by the expert system, these descriptions characterize a social system (how the expert interacts with his environment), not processes within an individual agent;

- Knowledge-level descriptions have an open interpretation, dependent on the point of view of the observer of the representation;
- Knowledge-level descriptions are always expressed in perceptual space, that is, they are themselves perceivable;
- The human expert, despite often being a theoretician of his own behavior, has no such notations; designing knowledge representations is the province of the knowledge engineer and AI researcher.

Perhaps now we can understand some of Newell's surprising comments about the knowledge level [Newell 1982] (*with my reinterpretations*):

The knowledge level is not realized as a state-like physical structure, "running counter to the common feature at all levels of a passive medium" (p. 105). *A knowledge-level description is an observer's description and explanation for how a situated system interacts with its environment; it does not correspond to physical structures stored and manipulated inside isolated agents.*

Knowledge can only be "imagined as the result of interpretive processes operating on symbolic expressions" (p. 105). *Knowledge is generated by the process of commenting on (representing) the meaning of perceived ("symbol level") structures.*

"It seems preferable to avoid calling the body of knowledge a memory" (p. 101). "The total system (i.e., the dyad of the observing and the observed agents) runs without there being any physical structure that is the knowledge" (p. 107). *Intelligent behavior isn't physically produced from internal, hidden knowledge representations; it creates them out where they can be seen or heard, interprets them, and is organized by this process.*

"Knowledge of the world cannot be captured in a finite structure" (p. 107). "Knowledge can only be created dynamically in time" (p. 108). *Knowledge is generated by an observer, relative to his point of view, in the process of making sense (modeling).*

"One way of viewing the knowledge level is as the attempt to build as good a model of an agent's behavior as possible based on information external to the agent" (p. 109). *The knowledge engineer's knowledge-level description of the expert emphasizes the expert's awareness and use of materials and circumstances in the environment; that is, it accounts for behavior in terms of interaction between agent and environment.*

As Newell says, knowledge can be represented, but it is never actually in hand. Each statement by the observer captures what he needs to say at any point in time, and each such statement is later interpretable in different ways. Subtle distinctions beyond the scope of this essay are required to further sort out Newell's statements. In particular, when the observer is describing an intelligent agent, a distinction needs to be drawn between knowledge as a capacity ascribed to the agent (dynamically changing through interaction with the environment, not necessarily existing as physical representations for the agent himself) and the observer's representations of this knowledge (perceivable structures, open for interpretation). Hence, we may be ready to return to and build upon Ryle's famous distinction between knowing how (a capacity to perform some action) and knowing that (a representation), in which the capacity to perform cannot be reduced to knowledge-level descriptions about it.

3. Reformulated Research Program

What are the implications for machine learning and knowledge acquisition if knowledge cannot be stored? First, we must adopt a different way of talking about our programs. As I have outlined above, the terms "model-based" and "qualitative reasoning" have been too restrictively applied to qualitative simulation. Adopting the systems-modeling perspective suggests that other approaches should be freely integrated (e.g., linear programming, Bayesian statistics), for we seek whatever models are useful for the task at hand. We are not modeling structures in the expert's head, though we will certainly continue to pay close attention to how he talks and what representations he uses (e.g., diagrams, notational shorthand, calculi). Most importantly, methods from cybernetics, general systems theory, and chaos theory for modeling situated systems need to be incorporated. For the most part, the knowledge engineering community has completely misconstrued the nature of classification and statistical models.

Second, researchers should commit to either providing practical knowledge acquisition tools or studying the nature of intelligence. Providing tools requires more careful attention to the social setting in which expert systems are used; this follows as a generalization and reapplication of the systems analysis given here, focusing on how teams of people interact to solve problems and how job aids can facilitate this interaction. Studying the nature of intelligence will surely continue to involve knowledge-level analyses, for this is the leverage that cognitive science provides over neurobiology. However, a clear separation should be made between knowledge-level descriptions and physical mechanisms. The idea that human-like intelligent behavior could be generated by interpreting stored programs that predescribe the world and ways of behaving must be abandoned, for this view confounds descriptions an observer might make with physical mechanisms inside the agent. Obviously, an agent's own observations, as representations about his situation, purposes, methods, etc., alter his behavior, but these representations are perceivable by the agent himself; they are not stored, matched, retrieved, and refiled by hidden processes [Clancey, in preparation]. Researchers can commit to both knowledge engineering and the study of intelligence, as surely both feed into each other. However, the practical needs of tool users and the difference between knowledge bases and the human mind require a more explicit commitment than before; otherwise, evaluation and choice of methods will be confused.

Finally, the machine learning community in general should attend to the lessons expressed here about how representations relate to human knowledge and make the same commitment required of the knowledge engineers. Much research remains to be done in developing automated methods for improving qualitative models, for example, using explanation-based learning. However, a distinction must be made between the syntactic methods that have been used to date (grammatically shuffling models of processes) and the kind of learning that occurs in the human brain each time a thought is expressed.

References

Bennett, J., Creary, L., Engelmore, R., and Melosh, R. 1978. SACON: A knowledge-based consultant for structural analysis. (STAN-CS-78-699 and HPP Memo 78-23). Stanford University, Stanford, CA.

Brown, J.S., Burton, R.R., and De Kleer, J. 1982. Pedagogical, natural language, and knowledge engineering techniques in SOPHIE I, II, and III. In D. Sleeman and J.S. Brown (Eds.), *Intelligent tutoring systems*. London: Academic Press.

Clancey. W.J. 1983. The advantages of abstract control knowledge in expert system design. *Proceedings of the National Conference on Artificial Intelligence* (pp. 74-78).

Clancey, W.J. 1985. Heuristic classification. *Artificial Intelligence*, 27, 289-350.

Clancey, W.J. 1989. Viewing knowledge bases as qualitative models. *IEEE Expert*, 4, 9-23.

Clancey, W.J. (in preparation). The frame of reference problem in the design of intelligent machines. In K. vanLehn (Ed.), *Architectures for intelligence: The twenty-second Carnegie symosium on cognition*. Hillsdale: Lawrence Erlbaum Associates.

Newell, A. 1982. The knowledge level. *Artificial Intelligence*, 18, 87-127.

Machine Learning, 4, 293–336 (1989)

Automated Knowledge Acquisition for Strategic Knowledge

THOMAS R. GRUBER   GRUBER@SUMEX-AIM.STANFORD.EDU
Knowledge Systems Laboratory, Computer Science Department, Stanford University, Stanford, CA 94305

Abstract. *Strategic knowledge* is used by an agent to decide what action to perform next, where actions have consequences external to the agent. This article presents a computer-mediated method for acquiring strategic knowledge. The general knowledge acquisition problem and the special difficulties of acquiring strategic knowledge are analyzed in terms of *representation mismatch*: the difference between the form in which knowledge is available from the world and the form required for knowledge systems. ASK is an interactive knowledge acquisition tool that elicits strategic knowledge from people in the form of *justifications* for action choices and generates *strategy rules* that operationalize and generalize the expert's advice. The basic approach is demonstrated with a human–computer dialog in which ASK acquires strategic knowledge for medical diagnosis and treatment. The rationale for and consequences of specific design decisions in ASK are analyzed, and the scope of applicability and limitations of the approach are assessed. The paper concludes by discussing the contribution of knowledge representation to automated knowledge acquisition.

Key Words. knowledge acquisition, knowledge engineering, human–computer interaction, strategic knowledge, knowledge representation

1. Introduction

Knowledge acquisition is the transfer and transformation of knowledge from the forms in which it is available in the world into forms that can be used by a knowledge system (adapted from [Buchanan, et al. 1983]). In the context of this article, knowledge in the world comes from people and knowledge in the system is implemented with formal symbol structures—knowledge representations. Knowledge acquisition is a multifaceted problem that encompasses many of the technical problems of knowledge engineering, the enterprise of building knowledge systems. Deciding what knowledge can be brought to bear for a problem, how the knowledge can be used by a program, how to represent it, and then eliciting it from people and encoding it in a knowledge base are all aspects of the knowledge acquisition problem. The inherent difficulty of these tasks makes knowledge acquisition a fundamental obstacle to the widespread use of knowledge system technology.

The research reported here addresses the problem of acquiring strategic knowledge from people. In particular, the article presents an approach by which an interactive computer program assists with the knowledge acquisition process. The general term *automated knowledge acquisition* refers to computer-mediated elicitation and encoding of knowledge from people.

The first section of this article provides a theoretical analysis of the general knowledge acquisition problem and introduces the problem of acquiring strategic knowledge. Section 2 reviews the techniques of automated knowledge acquisition in terms of the theoretical

47

framework developed in the first section and motivates the present work. Section 3 describes the automated knowledge acquisition tool called ASK. Section 4 demonstrates the program with a human–computer dialog. Sections 5, 6, and 7 provide an analysis of the scope of applicability, assumptions, and limitations of the system, and a discussion of key design decisions. A concluding section summarizes the contribution of the design of knowledge representations to the development of knowledge acquisition tools.

1.1. The Knowledge Acquisition Problem as Representation Mismatch

Most knowledge systems are built by knowledge engineers rather than by the domain experts who provide the knowledge. A long-standing goal of a course of knowledge acquisition research has been to replace the knowledge engineer with a program that assists in the direct "transfer of expertise" from experts to knowledge bases [Davis 1976]. Yet the problem has eluded a general solution; no existing knowledge acquisition program can build a knowledge system directly from experts' descriptions of what they do.

Why is knowledge acquisition difficult to automate? It seems that the "transfer" metaphor is misleading. Clearly, the form in which knowledge is available from people (e.g., descriptions in natural language) is different from the form in which knowledge is represented in knowledge systems. The difference between the two forms of knowledge, called *representation mismatch* [Buchanan, et al. 1983], is central to the problem of knowledge acquisition. Because of representation mismatch, one cannot merely transfer knowledge from human to machine. The knowledge acquisition tool must actively elicit knowledge in a form that can be obtained from domain experts and map elicited knowledge into the executable representations of the knowledge system. The mapping is difficult to automate because the requirements for building a working system (e.g., operationality, consistency) differ from the requirements for a human expert describing a procedure to another person. In order to automate knowledge acquisition, one must provide a method for overcoming representation mismatch.

The following discussion introduces three aspects of representation mismatch—modeling, operationalization, and generalization—as an explanatory framework with which to understand the problem of knowledge acquisition. The general issues and the specific problems of acquiring strategic knowledge are described within this framework.

1.1.1. Dimensions of Representation Mismatch   The *modeling* or formalization problem is a fundamental kind of representation mismatch. A knowledge system can be thought of as a qualitative model of systems in the world, including systems of intelligent activity [Clancey 1989]. While the model embodied by a knowledge system is informed by the behavior of human experts, it is not designed as a model of the experts' knowledge or their cognitive processes [Winograd and Flores 1986]. From this point of view, knowledge acquisition is a creative rather than imitative activity, resulting in a computational model that makes distinctions and abstractions not present in the initial language of the expert. Because of the difference between descriptions of behavior and computational models of action, the task of knowledge acquisition requires a model-building effort beyond that of rendering the expert's utterances in formal notation. Morik [1988] illustrates the modeling problem with the example of building a natural language-understanding system. The builder of such

a system does not interview experts in natural language understanding (native speakers) but experts in modeling the formal structure and mechanisms of language (linguists). Furthermore, the system-builder must adapt the expert's concepts (a theory of syntax) to the needs of a computational model (a parser) and sometimes invent new concepts (semantic networks).

The *operationalization* aspect of representation mismatch refers to the difference between descriptions of what the system should accomplish, given by domain experts, and the operational methods for achieving those objectives required by a computer program. Two senses of operationalization have been identified in the machine learning literature: making advice executable [Mostow 1983] or more useful [Keller 1988].[1] Knowledge acquisition involves both kinds of operationalization in the service of performance goals such as recommending an effective drug therapy or designing an efficient electric motor. To make a therapy recommendation executable, a knowledge engineer might build an interface that justifies a recommendation and requests the results. To make the advice "minimize cost, maximize speed" more useful, the engineer might decide to use a redesign algorithm and elicit more knowledge from the expert about ways to cut costs and fine tune performance by modifying existing designs. The methods in which expert-supplied specifications are operationalized may require concepts and terminology unfamiliar to the domain expert.

A third dimension of representation mismatch is *generalization*: the difference between a set of specific examples of desired input/output performance and a more concise representation that will enable a system to perform correctly on a larger class of input situations. It is frequently observed that it is much easier to elicit examples of expert problem solving than general rules or procedures that cover the examples. The available form of knowledge (classified examples) needs to be mapped into a more useful representation (general class descriptions).

Problems of modeling, operationalization, and generalization are ubiquitous in knowledge acquisition. We will now see how they are manifest in the case of a particular kind of knowledge, strategic knowledge.

1.2. The Problem of Acquiring Strategic Knowledge

1.2.1. Strategic Knowledge. *Strategic knowledge* is knowledge used by an agent to decide what action to perform next, where actions can have consequences external to the agent. The more general term *control knowledge* refers to knowledge used to decide what to do next. What constitutes an action and its consequences depends on how one characterizes what the agent can *do*. For knowledge systems that make recommendations to people (e.g., "increase dosage of drug D") or control physical systems (e.g., "close valve V"), actions have consequences that are observable in the world outside of the agent. For problem-solving programs based on state–space search, an action may be the firing of a rule or an operator. For such an agent, *search-control knowledge* is used to choose internal actions that increase the likelihood of reaching a solution state and improve the speed of computation. The research reported here distinguishes knowledge for deciding among actions with consequences in the external world because the goal is to acquire strategic knowledge from domain experts without reference to the symbol-level organization of the knowledge system.

For descriptive purposes, strategic knowledge is also distinguished from the *substantive knowledge* of a domain, knowledge about what is believed to be true in the world. Both substantive and strategic knowledge underlie expertise in many domains. For example, a robot uses substantive knowledge to recognize and interpret situations in the world (e.g., an obstacle in its path) and strategic knowledge to decide what to do (to go around or over it). A lawyer uses substantive knowledge to identify the relevant features of cases and strategic knowledge to decide which case to cite in defense of an argument. A diagnostician uses substantive knowledge to evaluate evidence pro and con hypotheses and uses strategic knowledge to decide among therapeutic actions. In general, substantive knowledge is used to identify relevant states of the world, and strategic knowledge is used to evaluate the utility of possible actions given a state.

1.2.2. Representation Mismatch for Strategic Knowledge

Although progress has been made in automating the acquisition of substantive knowledge used in classification [e.g., Bareiss 1989; Boose and Bradshaw 1987; Eshelman 1988], strategic knowledge is typically imparted to systems by knowledge engineers using implementation-level mechanisms. The difficulty of acquiring strategic knowledge directly from experts can be seen within the framework of the three aspects of representation mismatch introduced earlier.

First, strategic knowledge presents serious modeling problems. While substantive knowledge might be acquired in a perspicuous form, such as rules mapping evidence to hypotheses, strategic knowledge about choosing actions is often represented with programming constructs, such as procedures or agenda mechanisms. At least in principle, rules that encode substantive knowledge can be written in a process-independent context; experts can specify how to classify situations in the world without worrying about the mechanism by which the specifications are interpreted. However, specifying knowledge that affects the order and choice of actions involves building a computational model of a process.

Consider the problem of modeling the strategy of a medical *workup*: the process of gathering data, assessing the results, and planning treatment for an individual patient. Although medical diagnosis is often described as a static classification problem (i.e., to classify *given* data), in medical practice evidence for a diagnosis is gathered over time, and the actions that produce evidence are chosen strategically. In modeling the workup, requests for patient data, laboratory tests, diagnostic procedures, and options for trial therapy are treated as actions. Substantive knowledge is used for the classification task, identifying likely causes for a given set of findings. In addition, strategic knowledge is used to decide what action to take next when the data are not all in.

In the MYCIN system, much of the knowledge that determined question ordering and decisions about laboratory tests was represented with screening clauses, clause ordering, and "certainty factor engineering"—implementation-level manipulations of the rules to achieve the intended strategic behavior [Clancey 1983a]. This knowledge could not be acquired easily with the available rule editors and debugging support tools [Buchanan and Shortliffe 1984] because the strategy was implicit in the engineering tricks rather than the content of the rules. Since MYCIN, more explicit representations of strategic knowledge have been devised, such as the control blocks of S.1 [Erman, Scott, and London 1984] and the high-level control languages of BB1 [Hayes-Roth, et al. 1987]. Because these advances are general-purpose languages for control, rendering strategic knowledge in a computational model remains a programming task.

The acquisition of strategic knowledge also highlights the operationalization aspect of representation mismatch. At the *knowledge level* [Newell 1982], the strategic knowledge of an agent may be specified as a set of behavioral goals that the agent should attempt to achieve. While it is possible to elicit specifications of desired behavior at the knowledge level from experts, it is far more difficult for experts (and knowledge engineers) to specify *how* a knowledge system should achieve these goals.

For example, during conventional knowledge acquisition for a knowledge system called MUM [Cohen, et al. 1987], knowledge engineers interviewed a practicing physician for the purpose of modeling his diagnostic strategy for patients reporting chest and abdominal pain. MUM's task was to *generate* workups for chest pain patients, choosing one action at a time, waiting for the outcome of previous action. When asked to describe how to choose diagnostic tests, the expert would mention goals such as "do the cheap, quick tests first" and "protect the patient against a dangerous disease." This is nonoperational advice. To make it operational requires specifying how actions achieve goals (e.g., the diagnostic and therapeutic effect of actions), how to determine the currently relevant goals (e.g., when is a dangerous disease suspected), and how to balance competing objectives (e.g., cost, timeliness, diagnostic power, therapeutic value).

Third, the generalization aspect of representation mismatch is exhibited by the problem of acquiring strategic knowledge. By definition, experts are good at what they do; it does not follow that they are good at generalizing what they do. In particular, it is much easier to elicit *cases* of strategic decisions—choices among actions in specific situations—than to elicit general strategies.

For example, in the MUM domain of chest pain workups, the physician makes a series of decisions about actions. He typically starts with a set of questions about patient history, then performs a physical examination (in a knowledge system, steps in the examination are also implemented as requests for data), and then plans and executes a series of diagnostic tests and trial therapeutic actions, until sufficient evidence for a conclusive diagnosis or recommended therapy has been found. For MUM it was feasible to elicit example workups corresponding to actual patients. These workups can be viewed as very specific plans. Each step in the workup, each choice of what to ask to try next, is the result of a strategic decision. However, generalizations about classes of strategic decisions were not present in the original workup descriptions but developed by retrospective analysis of the cases and follow-up consultation with the expert. Within a single workup there may be several actions chosen for the same reasons (e.g., "do the cheap, quick tests first"), and there may be common reasons across workups (e.g., "gather enough evidence to recommend therapy").

Although cases of specific workups can be acquired in the form of directed graphs, they are not general enough for a knowledge system. First, they are specific to individual patients, and workups differ over individuals. Second, these plan-like procedures are extremely brittle; if any action cannot be taken (e.g., because the results of a test are not available), then the procedures fail. Third, because they only record the results of strategic decisions, workup graphs fail to capture the underlying reasons for selecting actions in the prescribed order. This third problem reveals a subtle form of representation mismatch: although it is possible to elicit reasons for past strategic decisions, these reasons alone do not constitute a *generative* strategy. A generative strategy plans new workups based on the strategic knowledge that gave rise to existing workups.

The work reported in this article is motivated by the problem of acquiring knowledge that underlies strategic decisions and putting it in operational, general form. The next section lays out some of the techiques for addressing the problem.

2. Techniques for Overcoming Representation Mismatch

Interactive tools can assist with knowledge acquisition by overcoming representation mismatch. This section reviews the techniques used by existing knowledge acquisition tools and motivates the approach taken in ASK. The techniques are presented in the context of the three aspects of representation mismatch.

2.1. Incorporating Models into Knowledge Acquisition Tools

Conventionally, the modeling problem for knowledge acquisition is handled by the knowledge engineer, who is responsible for building the knowledge system. The engineer analyzes the *performance task* (the problem to be solved by the knowledge system) and designs a program for applying knowledge to perform the task. A performance task is defined in terms of the input and output requirements of the system and the knowledge that is available. Tasks can be described at multiple levels of abstraction, from the functional specifications for a single application to input/output requirements for a general class of tasks. A *problem solving method* is the technique by which a knowledge system brings specific knowledge to bear on the task. When the computational requirements and methods for a *class* of tasks are well understood, a domain-independent problem-solving method can be designed, such as heuristic classification [Chandrasekaran 1983; Clancey 1985].

A *task-level architecture* consists of a knowledge representation language (a set of representational primitives) and a procedure implementing the problem-solving method designed to support knowledge systems for a class of performance tasks [Chandrasekaran 1986; Gruber and Cohen 1987]. The procedure, which in this article is called the *method* for short, is a mechanism by which knowledge stated in the architecture's knowledge representation is applied to perform one of the tasks in the abstract class of tasks for which the architecture is designed. The representation and the method of a task-level architecture are tightly coupled. Each method defines *roles* for knowledge: ways in which knowledge is applied by the method [McDermott 1988]. The algorithm that implements the method in a program operates on statements in the associated representation language. The primitive terms in the representation correspond to the roles of knowledge. For example, Chandrasekaran [1987] and his colleagues have built architectures for *generic tasks* such as hierarchical classification and routine design. Each generic task is described in terms of the function to be performed (an abstract description of the performance task), a knowledge representation language (the set of primitive terms), and a control strategy (the procedure that implements the method). Chandrasekaran uses the term *generic task problem solvers* to refer to task-level architectures.

Task-level architectures can facilitate knowledge acquisition. Like a virtual machine, the architecture supports a set of method-specific representation primitives for building a knowledge system. Much of the model-building effort can be put into the design of the architecture, and the representational primitives can hide the implementation details. As a consequence, the architecture can reduce representation mismatch by presenting a task-level representation language comprehensible to the domain expert [Bylander and Chandrasekaran 1987; Gruber and Cohen 1987; Musen 1989].

Interactive knowledge acquisition tools can help overcome representation mismatch by employing special techniques for eliciting and analyzing knowledge in architecture-supported representations. Some tools help analyze the task requirements to choose among existing methods and instantiate an architecutre with domain terminology. For example, ROGET [Bennett 1985] offers help in choosing among a small set of particular heuristic classification methods and elicits domain-specific instantiations of the input, output, and intermediate concepts for the selected method.

Other tools specialize in eliciting the knowledge for the roles required by the problem-solving method. For example MOLE [Eshelman 1988] uses an instantiation of the heuristic classification method called cover-and-differentiate. The knowledge acquisition tool specializes in the elicitation of knowledge for roles such as "covering knowledge" and "differentiating knowledge." Similarly, SALT [Marcus 1988] is based on the propose-and-revise method for constructive problem solving, and elicits knowledge for proposing design extensions, identifying constraints, and backtracking from violated constraints.

Tools of another category specialize in a particular formulation of knowledge, independent of how the knowledge will be applied to particular tasks. For example, repertory grid tools elicit knowledge in the form of a two-dimensional matrix of weighted associations between "elements" and "traits" [Boose and Bradshaw 1987; Shaw and Gaines 1987]. These tools use a task-independent elicitation technique to help the user identify traits and elements and the strengths of associations among them and provides detailed analyses of the information. The user interprets the feedback in terms of a particular task, such as a procurement decision or an evaluation of policy alternatives.

On the other end of the spectrum are elicitation tools that are customized to the problem-solving method and a specific task in a domain. An example is OPAL, which acquires protocols used in the domain of cancer therapy [Musen, Fagan, Combs, and Shortliffe 1987]. The problem-solving method is a kind of skeletal-plan refinement, and the performance task is to manage cancer-therapy protocols modeled as skeletal plans. OPAL elicits knowledge from experts entirely in domain-specific terms and in forms that correspond to paper and pencil representations familiar to the experts. Because the tool has almost completely eliminated the representation mismatch due to modeling, it has been used successfully by physicians with little experience with computation [Musen 1989].

The acquisition of strategic knowledge, as it has been defined, is not supported by conventional task-level architectures. In fact, all of the built-in methods of the architectures mentioned above are implemented with procedures that themselves encode a control strategy. To the extent that the strategy is implemented by the method, it cannot be acquired by tools that assume the method is fixed.

However, it is possible to design an architecture for a restricted class of tasks that require domain-specific strategic knowledge. The method for such an architecture should define roles for strategic knowledge, just as MOLE's method defines roles for substantive knowledge, such as knowledge for proposing explanations that cover an abnormal symptom. As will be described in Section 3, ASK was designed with an architecture that represents strategic knowledge as rules that map situations to desired actions. In this architecture, strategic knowledge is limited to three roles for associating features in the agent's current model of the world with classes of appropriate actions. As will be discussed in Section 6, the restricted roles for strategic knowledge reduce the scope of what needs to be acquired and simplify how elicited knowledge is operationalized and generalized. They also limit the class of strategies that can be acquired.

2.2. Eliciting Knowledge in Operational Terms

Automated knowledge acquisition tools can address the operationalization aspect of representation mismatch by limiting what is elicited from the user to representations of knowledge that are already machine-executable—that is, to elicit knowledge in the form in which it will be used for performance or in some form that can be compiled into the runtime representation. An alternative approach is to provide a nonoperational "mediating representation" for eliciting the conceptual structure of a domain and then *manually* building a system that operationalizes the specifications [Johnson and Tomlinson 1988]. A rule editor is a simple example of a tool that elicits knowledge in a form that can be directly executed.

The technique of eliciting knowledge directly in executable form is reminiscent of the single representation trick [Dietterich, et al. 1982] in which the learning agent is given training data in the same representation as the language used for describing learned concepts. Using this technique in a knowledge acquisition tool replaces the problem of making the elicited input executable (operationalization) with the assumption that the elicitation language is representationally adequate. A language is representationally adequate if all of the relevant domain knowledge can be stated in the representation.

The success of tools employing this technique depends in part on whether the elicitation interface can make the operational semantics of the representation comprehensible to the user. For example, although TEIRESIAS paraphrases rules into English, the user needs to know more than English to understand them. TEIRESIAS depends on the assumption that the user can understand the backward-chaining model [Davis 1976].

Well-designed user interface techniques can help make the computational model of the architecture comprehensible to the user. For example, the OPAL tool facilitates the acquisition of cancer treatment protocols with a form-filling interface, emulating paper-and-pencil forms familiar to its users [Musen, et al. 1987]. Similarly, spreadsheet applications are made comprehensible by presenting a familiar metaphor. The interface design goal is to minimize the conceptual distance between the user's understanding of the system's mechanism and the system's presentation of the options afforded by the computational model [Hutchins, Hollan, and Norman 1986].

A tool that acquires knowledge in an executable representation can also offer intelligent assistance by analyzing the consequences of *applying* the knowledge. For example, SALT elicits fine-grained rules for repairing local constraint violations in a design task. One of the consequences of using backtracking from local constraint violations is that the user can unintentionally define cycles in the dependency network, in which repairing one constraint violation introduces another. SALT can analyze the elicited knowledge, identify cycles, and offer assistance to the user in specifying different routes for backtracking [Marcus 1987].

It is difficult to acquire strategic knowledge in executable form without forcing the expert to understand symbol-level mechanisms such as procedures and priority schemes. There is a tension between the requirement to provide the user with a language that is comprehensible and yet sufficiently powerful to implement the strategy. There are some techniques that help elicit specifications of control, such as visual programming interfaces for building transition networks [Musen, Fagan, and Shortliffe 1986] and graph-drawing tools for specifying decision trees [Hannan and Politakis 1986]. However, the strategic knowledge that can generate decisions among actions is *implicit* in transition networks and decision trees.

ASK's representation of strategic knowledge was designed to correspond to the form in which experts can describe their strategic knowledge: justifications for specific actions in specific situations. As will be explained in Section 3, ASK elicits justifications for choices among actions in terms of features of strategic situations and actions. ASK's design ensures that the features mentioned in justifications are operational; the features are well-defined functions and relations that hold over objects in a knowledge base representing the current state of problem solving.

Like all tools that elicit knowledge in executable form, ASK is based on the assumption of representational adequacy discussed above. There are two ways this assumption can fail: the computational model is inadequate for describing the desired strategy, or the set of terms in the existing knowledge representation is incomplete. The former problem is a function of the architecture, as discussed above. The problem of incomplete terms can be handled in an interactive tool if the user is given the chance to define new terms with the representational primitives provided by the architecture.

Since defining terms for a knowledge system is an operationalization task, it is a challenge to provide automated assistance. A promising approach is exemplified by PROTÉGÉ, a tool that helps the knowledge engineer define domain-specific instantiations of architecture-level representational primitives [Musen 1989]. PROTÉGÉ generates OPAL-class elicitation tools meant for the domain expert in which the vocabulary is fixed. ASK provides a means for defining new features in the context of eliciting justifications, as demonstrated in Section 4.6. By design, ASK integrates the acquisition of new features and the acquisition of knowledge that uses the features.

2.3. Integrating Mechanical Generalization with Interactive Knowledge Elicitation

Machine learning techniques are an obvious answer to the generalization aspect of representation mismatch. There are many well-established techniques for generalization from examples [Dieterich and Michalski 1983]. Because inductive generalization is inherently underconstrained, these techniques all depend on some kind of *bias* to direct the learner toward useful or relevant generalizations [Mitchell 1982; Utgoff 1986]. Bias can be provided to a learner by supplying a highly constrained generalization space, defined by the language for representing learned concepts, such as LEX's pattern-matching language [Mitchell, Utgoff, and Banerji 1983]. Bias can also come from the choice of features in the training examples, as in the feature vectors used by decision tree algorithms [Quinlan 1986].

A knowledge acquisition tool can capitalize on existing techniques if they are augmented with the appropriate bias. One approach would be to build the necessary bias into the tool.

If the bias is itself important domain knowledge, however, this approach limits the usefulness of automating the knowledge acquisition process, since the tool would have to be modified for each domain. Instead, a knowledge acquisition tool can provide means for the *user* to contribute bias—to guide the generalization toward useful concepts. The user can contribute bias by carefully selecting training examples [Winston 1985], by identifying their relevant features, and by evaluating machine-generated generalizations. While the human provides pedagogical input and evaluation of results, the tool can apply syntactic generalization operators and check for consistency with a database of training cases. The resulting human-machine synergy is a more powerful acquisition technique than either manual knowledge engineering or traditional inductive learning.

Knowledge-based learning techniques such as explanation-based learning [DeJong and Mooney 1986; Mitchell, Keller, and Kedar-Cabelli 1986] are strongly biased by the domain theory provided by the system builder. Inserting a human in the learning loop can help overcome the dependence of the learning technique on the quality of the built-in knowledge. For example, in an experiment with SOAR in the domain of algebraic simplification, a human intercedes during problem solving to help the system learn search-control knowledge [Golding, Rosenbloom, and Laird 1987]. When the system needs to choose among algebraic simplification operators for a specific equation, the human recommends an operator to apply or provides a simpler equation to solve. The system uses a domain theory of algebraic simplification to find useful chunks that generalize the situation (the class of equations) in which the recommended operator should be applied. In the absence of a complete domain theory, one can imagine the human pointing out relevant parts of the equation to chunk.

To integrate generalization techniques into a knowledge acquisition tool, the knowledge to be acquired must be represented in such a way that syntactic generalizations of statements in the representation correspond to semantic generalizations in the knowledge [see Lenat and Brown 1984]. For strategic knowledge, this means formulating the selection of actions in terms of classification. For example, a common technique for programs that learn search-control knowledge is to formulate the knowledge for selecting actions as pattern-matching expressions that identify situations in which operators would be usefully applied [Benjamin 1987; Laird, Newell, and Rosenbloom 1987; Minton and Carbonell 1987; Mitchell, Utgoff, and Banerji 1983; Silver 1986]. Because of this formulation, syntactic generalizations of the expressions to which an operator had been applied during training correspond to classes of situations where the operator might be useful in the future.

ASK's representation of strategic knowledge is designed to exploit syntactic generalization operators. Knowledge about what action to do next is formulated as predicates that describe situations in which equivalence classes of actions are useful. In the absence of a theory to infer the utility of actions, ASK acquires strategic knowledge from people.

3. The ASK Knowledge Acquisition Assistant

ASK is an interactive knowledge acquisition assistant. It acquires strategic knowledge from the user of a knowledge system, called the performance system. The strategic knowledge acquired by ASK is used by the performance system to decide what action to perform on each iteration of a control cycle. With additional strategic knowledge, the performance system should be able to make better decisions about what to do in various situations.

The basic approach is to elicit strategic knowledge from the user in the form of *justifications* for specific choices among actions, and then operationalize and generalize the justified choices in the form of *strategy rules* that associate situations with classes of appropriate actions.

This section presents an overview of the knowledge acquisition procedure, and then covers in more detail the strategy-rule representation and the knowledge system architecture that supports it. Section 4 demonstrates ASK with examples from a knowledge system for planning workups of chest pain.

3.1. The Knowledge Acquisition Dialog

ASK orchestrates a mixed-initiative dialog with the user. The basic steps in the knowledge acquisition dialog are shown in Figure 1.

ASK is invoked by the user of the performance system. At run time, the performance system executes a simple control loop. On each iteration the system selects a set of recommended actions, the user picks one, and then the system executes it. The results of the actions are recorded, and then the system continues by selecting the next set of recommended actions. If the user disagrees with the system's recommended actions on any iteration, she can interrupt the control loop and initiate a knowledge acquisition dialog.

The first step of the knowledge acquisition dialog is to elicit a critique from the user. A critique is a labeling of what the system did wrong in terms of choosing actions. The system recommends a set of actions at each iteration of the control cycle because they are all equally appropriate in the current situation, according to the existing strategic knowledge. The user

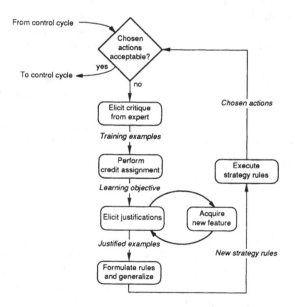

Figure 1. The ASK knowledge acquisition dialog.

critiques the system's choices by selecting an action that the system should have chosen (the positive example) and one that the system should not have chosen (the negative example). The positive and negative examples do not have to be in the set of the system's initial choices (which may be empty). The user also characterizes the system's error in recommending actions, indicating, for instance, whether the positive example is merely preferred to the negative example or whether the negative example should not have been considered at all.

Next, ASK performs credit assignment analysis by examining how the current set of strategy rules matched the positive and negative examples. The output of this analysis is a learning objective that specifies what a new strategy rule would have to match and not match and what it should recommend in order to accommodate the user's critique and be consistent with existing strategy rules.

Then ASK elicits justifications from the user. From the user's perspective, justifications are explanations or reasons why an action should or should not be recommended, in terms of relevant features of the current situation. From ASK's perspective, justifications are facts about the state of knowledge base objects in the current working memory of the performance system; the set of justifications corresponds to the set of features that should be mentioned in matching strategy rules. ASK suggests an initial seed set of justifications, based on how existing strategy rules fired. The user adds justifications by clicking on features of objects displayed in windows on the screen. The justification interface allows the user to browse through the knowledge base for relevant objects. If the set of existing features is inadequate, the user can define new features within the justification interface.

When the user indicates that she is finished and has specified a set of justifications that are sufficient to distinguish the positive and negative examples, ASK generates a new strategy rule from the justifications. The new strategy rule is generalized by syntactic induction operators to apply to a range of situations and an equivalence class of actions. For example, where a specific action appears in a justification, ASK puts a variable in the corresponding clause of a strategy rule. Similarly, if a justification mentions a specific value for a feature, ASK may build a strategy-rule clause that matches a *range* of values for that feature.

Finally the new rule is paraphrased and the operational effects of the new rule are presented to the user for approval. If the user agrees that the new rule improves the system's choices of actions, the rule is added to the strategic knowledge base of the performance system, and the control cycle is continued.

Details of the knowledge acquisition dialog are demonstrated with examples in Section 4. First some background on the performance system architecture and the representation for strategic knowledge is required.

3.2. The MU Architecture

ASK is integrated with an architecture for knowledge systems called MU [Cohen, Greenberg, and Delisio 1987; Gruber and Cohen 1987]. As depicted in Figure 2, a performance system built in MU consists of a substantive knowledge base, typically for heuristic classification, and a strategic knowledge base for controlling actions.[2] This division of knowledge is typical of architectures that support control knowledge, such as BB1 [Hayes-Roth 1985]. MU organizes the substantive knowledge as a symbolic inference network, where inferences are

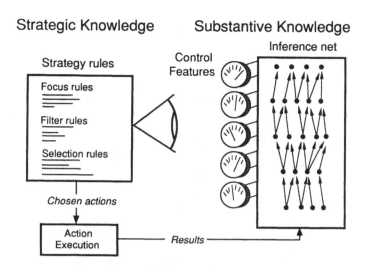

Figure 2. The MU architecture with strategy rules.

propagated from evidence to hypotheses by local combination functions. The inference network serves as the working memory of the system at runtime. The state of the network is abstracted by *control features*, which are functions, attributes, and relations over knowledge base objects.[2] The strategic knowledge is organized in a separate component, which examines the state of working memory via control features and selects actions to execute. MU was designed to support a variety of experiments in strategic reasoning, so the architecture does not include a built-in problem solving method or control strategy. The strategy-rule representation was developed for the study of knowledge acquisition in ASK.

3.3. Strategy Rules

Strategic knowledge acquired by ASK is represented in the form of *strategy rules*, inspired by the metarules that represent diagnostic strategy in NEOMYCIN and HERACLES [Clancey 1988; Clancey and Bock 1988]. Strategy rules map *strategic situations* to sets of recommended actions. Strategic situations are states of the working memory of a performance system. In the MU architecture, strategic situations are states of the inference network.

The strategy-rule control cycle, shown in Figure 3, specifies how strategy rules are applied in a performance system to decide among actions. At each iteration of the control cycle, strategy rules recommend the actions that are appropriate to perform next. There are three types of recommendations, corresponding to three categories of strategy rules. *Focus rules* propose a set of possible actions at each iteration. *Filter rules* prune actions that violate constraints. *Selection rules* pick out subsets of the proposed and unpruned actions that are most desirable in the current situation to form the final set of recommended actions. One of the actions in the recommended set is chosen by the user and executed. The effects of executing the action are then propagated through working memory.

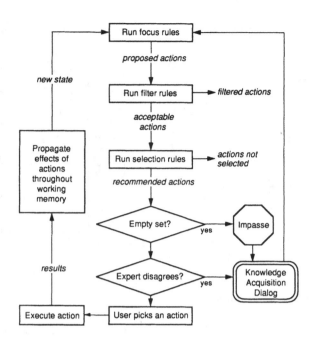

Figure 3. The strategy rule control cycle.

The strategy-rule control cycle corresponds to the method of task-level architectures described in Section 2.1. It specifies how strategic knowledge is brought to bear in the decision about what action to do next. The propose-filter-select algorithm defines three roles for strategic knowledge: specifying the conditions under which actions might be applicable, inappropriate, and preferable. Its design stipulates that actions are chosen iteratively, waiting for the effects of the execution of the previous action before making the current decision. The algorithm also assumes that the context of the decision, the *strategic situation*, is defined in terms of currently available features of the state of the performance system. Thus, strategy rules are *not* general-purpose control rules, useful for writing arbitrary programs. Rather, the strategy-rule control cycle supports a style of reasoning that has been called *reactive planning* [Agre and Chapman 1987; Chapman and Agre 1987; Firby 1987; Kaelbling 1987]. The form of strategic knowledge is restricted to facilitate automated knowledge acquisition. The consequences of this design are made explicit in later sections.

The left-hand side (If part) of a strategy rule is a conjunctive expression, with variables, that specifies a strategic situation and the set of recommended actions for that situation. The left-hand side expression matches against the values of control features that reflect the properties and dynamic state of objects in working memory, including objects that represent actions. The right-hand side (Then part) of a strategy rule indicates whether the matching actions should be proposed, filtered, or selected in the matching situation.

3.4. Examples from the Chest Pain Domain

Here are some examples of strategy rules and control features from a system for planning workups for chest pain that will be used to demonstrate ASK in Section 4.

The following *focus rule* proposes actions that are general questions (e.g., age, sex, etc.) when the set of active hypotheses, called the differential, is empty.

```
Rule Ask-intake-questions   a focus rule
   ''Ask general questions when at a loss.''
If: (IS (differential) :EMPTY)
     (IN ?ACTION (members-of general-questions))
Then: (PROPOSE ?action history-and-exam)
```

The strategic situation in this rule is specified by the condition that the value of the dif-ferential object is empty. The set of recommended actions is generated by the relation members-of applied to the object general-questions, which is a class of actions. The right-hand side operator PROPOSE specifies that the values bound to the variable ?ACTION should be proposed under these conditions, and that the goal history-and-exam should be posted.

The expression (differential) refers to the set of hypotheses on the differential. It is a control feature defined in the MU inference network as:

```
VALUE of DIFFERENTIAL               a control feature
   ''The set of active hypotheses''
SET-OF ?Hypothesis IN hypotheses SUCH-THAT
   trigger-level OF ?Hypothesis IS triggered AND
   level-of-support OF ?Hypothesis IS-NOT disconfirmed
OR
   level-of-support OF ?Hypothesis IS-AT-LEAST supported
```

Another focus rule, shown below, is complementary to Ask-intake-questions. It proposes actions that potentially provide diagnostic evidence when the differential is *not* empty, and labels this state with the goal gather-evidence-for-differential.

```
Propose-diagnostic-evidence               a focus rule
   ''Gather evidence for current hypotheses.''
If: (IS (differential) :NONEMPTY)
     (IN ?ACTION (potential-evidence differential))
Then: (PROPOSE ?ACTION gather-evidence-for-differential)
```

The expression (potential-evidence differential) refers to a control feature that returns the set of actions that are potentially diagnostic for hypotheses on the differential. This set is computed dynamically by a function that calls a MU service for analyzing the inference network [Cohen, Greenberg and Delisio 1987].

A very simple *filter rule* prevents actions from being recommended if they have already been executed. In some domains actions may be executed repeatedly. That is why the don't-repeat policy is encoded in the following rule instead of built in to the basic control loop.

```
Filter-executed-actions              a filter rule
   ''Do not repeat actions''
If: (IS (executed? ?ACTION) yes)
Then: (FILTER ?ACTION)
```

The following *selection rule* is enabled under the goal history-and-exam. It recommends those actions that are cheap to perform and that can potentially produce data that would trigger new hypotheses.

```
Select-cheap-triggering-data              a selection rule
   ''Prefer cheap actions that might trigger hypotheses.''
If: (IN history-and-exam (current-goals))
    (IS (potentially-triggered-by ?ACTION) :NONEMPTY)
    (≤ (cost ?ACTION) cheap)
Then: (SELECT ?ACTION)
Shadows: Select-triggering-data, select-free-evidence,
          select-cheap-evidence
```

The terms current-goals, potentially-triggered-by, and cost refer to control features. The set of actions recommended by this rule are those with some hypotheses on their potentially-triggered-by feature and whose cost feature is not more than cheap. The feature potentially-triggered-by is computed from the definitions of triggering conditions for hypotheses, stated in a rule-like form. For example, the hypothesis classic-angina is triggered when "the chief-complaint is pain or pressure and pain-quality is vise-like and the chief-complaint-location is substernal." This rule will recommend the action of asking for the chief-complaint-location because it potentially triggers a hypothesis and it is cheap.

3.5. The Shadowing Relation Among Strategy Rules

Within each strategy-rule category (focus, filter, selection), rules are matched in an order specified by a precedence relation called *shadows*, which is a partial order based on the generality of left-hand sides. If a rule succeeds (matches some objects), then the more general rules that it shadows are pruned (prevented from being fired). Generality is defined in terms of the features mentioned in a rule and the range of values specified for each feature. For example, the selection rule shown above, Select-cheap-triggering-data, shadows (takes precedence over) more general rules mentioning the same features. It shadows the more general rule Select-cheap-evidence, which recommends any action that is cheap. In turn, Select-cheap-evidence shadows the rule Select-free-evidence because the former matches actions with costs of cheap *or* free. The global effect of a family of selection rules in which the more specific rules shadow the more general is to choose those actions judged to be acceptable by the most constraining criteria. The shadows relation is a symbolic alternative to a numeric function for combining the recommendations of each rule into a single measure of utility. Further details can be found in [Gruber 1989].

4. A Knowledge Acquisition Dialog with ASK

In this section, ASK will be demonstrated in the context of a performance system that generates diagnostic workups for patients reporting chest and abdominal pain. The performance system is a reimplementation of the MUM knowledge system [Cohen, et al. 1987]. MUM's task is called *prospective diagnosis*, which is to choose diagnostic actions as a physician would, asking questions in an intelligent order and balancing the potential costs of diagnostic tests and trial therapy with the evidential and therapeutic benefits.

4.1. What the Performance System Already Knows

In experiments with ASK, the performance system is given MUM's substantive knowledge about the diagnosis of chest pain, implemented in the MU architecture in an inference network. The inference network contains hypotheses, data-gathering actions, intermediate conclusions, and combination functions that represent inferential relations such as the evidential support for hypotheses given patient data. MUM's original strategy was written by knowledge engineers in Lisp. In the ASK experiments, the strategic knowledge is represented in strategy rules.

In the dialog shown here, the performance system starts with a small but incomplete set of strategy rules, and the user extends them to improve strategic performance. ASK can also be used without any existing strategy rules. In a separate experiment reported in [Gruber 1989], ASK was used to acquire a set of strategy rules that replicates the original MUM strategy. However, since ASK makes use of existing strategy rules and control features in acquiring new strategic knowledge, it can be more helpful in specializing an existing strategy than in building a strategy from scratch. Thus the dialog in this section will show ASK being used to extend an existing set of rules that represent a general strategy for prospective diagnosis.

4.2. Running the Performance System

A MU performance system runs the basic control loop that was introduced in Section 3.3. At each iteration, strategy rules recommend some set of actions as candidates. From the system's point of view, these recommended actions are equivalent. Given the current strategic knowledge, the system could select among them arbitrarily. The user of a MU system is given the choice to "break the tie" and pick one action to execute. In the chest pain application, executing an action typically causes a request for data (e.g., symptoms or test results). That data is entered into the inference network, where it may change the evidential support for active hypotheses and trigger new hypotheses.

We begin the knowledge acquisition dialog at a point at which the user has already run the performance system through the first several actions in a case (namely, the cheap and easy questions about the history and the physical examination data). At this point, the system has run out of cheap actions and the Propose-diagnostic-evidence rule (Section 3.4) recommends a set of diagnostic actions. The user has the option to pick one of the recommended actions for execution or to teach the system to refine its strategy.

The following menu shows the system offering a set of recommended actions during an iteration of the control cycle of the performance system. Instead of choosing an action, the user initiates the dialog with ASK to "teach the system to improve its choices." (An item with a box drawn around it signifies that the user has selected it with the mouse.) The user sets up this diagnostic situation because it demonstrates a weakness in the system's strategy. The system needs to be more selective in choosing among diagnostic tests and trial therapeutic actions such as the seven offered in the menu.

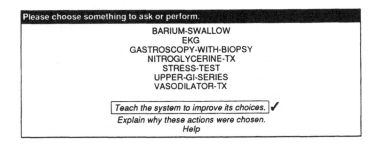

4.3. Eliciting the User's Critique

ASK elicits a critique from the user by presenting the list of the system's chosen actions and asking what should have been done differently. It first asks for the general category of error, to help determine whether the problem is with focus, filter, or selection rules:

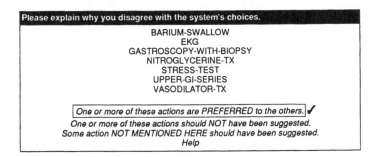

Then it asks for a positive example, an action that should have been recommended, and a negative example, an action that should not have been recommended. It is assumed that the user will choose a positive example that is representative of a class of actions that should be recommended in this situation, and a negative example that represents a class of actions to distinguish in this situation. In the interaction shown below, the user indicates that the action EKG should have been distinguished from the action Upper-GI-series, which is a reasonable alternative (i.e., a near miss).

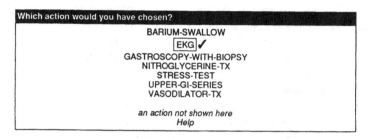

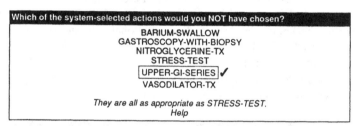

4.4. Credit Assignment Analysis

Using the information provided by the user, ASK performs a credit assignment analysis. The credit assignment algorithm examines how existing strategy rules matched in this situation and determines the requirements for a new rule that would account for the critique. The algorithm makes strong use of the distinction between focus, filter, and selection rules and the way they are applied in the strategy-rule control cycle. For example, if the positive example was not proposed by any focus rules, the algorithm prescribes learning a focus rule that proposes it. Alternatively, if both the positive and negative examples are recommended by selection rules, then the algorithm prescribes learning a selection rule that matches the positive example, fails to match the negative example, and shadows the selection rules that recommended the negative example. In the sample session, ASK determines that it needs to acquire a selection rule, specializing the Propose-diagnostic-evidence rule, such that the new rule matches EKG and does not match Upper-GI-series. The complete credit assignment algorithm can be found in [Gruber 1989].

4.5. Eliciting Justifications

In the next stage of the dialog, the user provides justifications for choosing the positive example over the negative example. Justifications are specified as features of the current strategic situation and features of actions. In the example session, the strategic situation is characterized by the state of hypotheses on the differential. A feature shared by the actions recommended by the system (including the positive and negative examples) is that they potentially provide evidence for hypotheses on the differential. In the current example, the user must provide additional justifications that distinguish the positive example EKG from the negative example Upper-GI-series.

The user interface for asserting justifications consists of two windows containing mouse-sensitive text. The "relevant objects window" displays the values of features of a set of objects from the knowledge base. The "justifications window" contains a list of justifications in the form of natural language sentences. Each justification is a description of the value of a feature of some relevant object.

ASK initializes the relevant objects window with a set of knowledge base objects that might be relevant to the current control decision. An object is considered relevant if it is one of the positive or negative examples (actions), a current goal, an instance of a class representing some aspect of the global state of the inference network, or if it is mentioned in a strategy rule matching the positive or negative examples. The user is provided with tools for browsing the knowledge base to find additional relevant objects.

ASK also initializes the list of statements in the justification window with *seed justifications* which represent the system's reasons for selecting the current actions. Seed justifications are derived from the clauses of strategy rules matching the positive and negative examples. In the windows shown below, objects and justifications have been seeded by ASK.

Objects Relevant to the Control Decision

CRITICAL-HYPOTHESES
    Value: classic-angina, unstable-angina
CURRENT-GOALS
    Value: gather-evidence-for-differential
DIFFERENTIAL
    Potential-evidence: barium-swallow, ekg, gastroscopy-with-biopsy, nitroglycerine-tx,
    Potentially-conclusive-evidence: barium-swallow, ekg, gastroscopy-with-biopsy, str
    Value: classic-angina, esophagitis, esophageal-reflux, pericarditis, unstable-angina,
EKG
    Applicability: APPLICABLE
    Classes: diagnostic-tests.
    Cost: LOW
    Executed?: NO
    Potentially-confirms: classic-angina, prinzmetal-angina, unstable-angina, variant-an
                     more below

Justifications for the Current Control Decision

GATHER-EVIDENCE-FOR-DIFFERENTIAL is in the CURRENT-GOALS.
EKG is in the POTENTIAL-EVIDENCE of DIFFERENTIAL.
UPPER-GI-SERIES is in the POTENTIAL-EVIDENCE of DIFFERENTIAL.

The user asserts a justification by selecting a feature of one of the objects presented in the relevant objects window. When a justification is selected, ASK paraphrases the fact in the justifications window. In the following interaction, the user indicates that EKG should have been chosen because it has low cost. Using the mouse, the user selects the statement "Cost: low" from the relevant objects window, and the statement "The COST of EKG is low" shows up in the justification window, as depicted below.

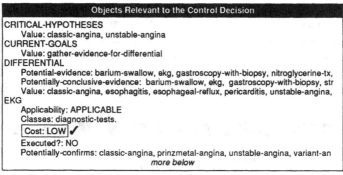

At this point the user could tell ASK that she was finished. If the set of justifications satisfied the learning objective, ASK would then turn the justifications into a new strategy rule. In this session, however, the user wishes to add more justifications. In particular, the user wants to say that EKG is appropriate in this situation not only because it has low cost, but also because it takes little time to perform. To be able to say this in the language of justifications, the user needs to define a new feature.

4.6. Acquiring a New Feature

To define a new feature is to implement an attribute, function, or relation over some set of objects in the knowledge base. ASK can help the user define a new feature. Playing the role of a knowledge engineer, ASK elicits the information needed to implement the feature in the MU architecture. The interaction below shows the user defining a new feature called "time required." The user starts by clicking on the EKG object in the relevant objects window, bringing up the following menu:

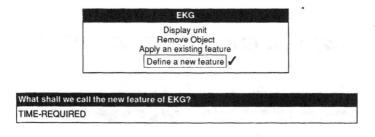

After obtaining a name for the feature, ASK needs to determine its general type. The type of a feature is a symbol-level property, dependent on the knowledge-base architecture. MU supports several varieties of control features, many of which are best implemented by knowledge engineers (e.g., dynamic relations written in Lisp). ASK knows about how features are implemented in MU and makes it possible to acquire some of the more simple features, such as static attributes, interactively. To help make architecture-dependent terms such as "inferential value" concrete to the user, ASK offers instances of features types from the current knowledge base as exemplars. In the menu below, the user indicates that the time-required feature is an attribute of actions, analogous to the cost feature.

> **What kind of feature is TIME-REQUIRED?**
>
> an attribute of actions (like COST) ✓
> a class of actions (like DIAGNOSTIC-TESTS)
> an object (like DIFFERENTIAL)
> an inferential value computed by rules (like LEVEL-OF-SUPPORT)
> a dynamic relation (like POTENTIALLY-CONFIRMS)
> *Help*

To complete the definition of a static attribute, ASK elicits information about the domain, data type, possible values, order, cardinality, and default value for the feature, and constrains the user's choices whenever possible.

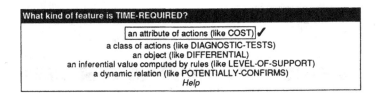

To which of these parent classes of EKG will Time-required apply?

Actions ⟷ Data ⟷ Diagnostic-tests ⟷ EKG

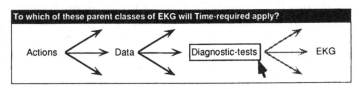

What possible values might Time-required take?

Yes or No (like EXECUTED? of EKG)
one of a list of words (like COST of EKG) ✓
a member of a KB class (like CURRENT-GOALS)
a number (like VALUE of AGE)
a duration of time (like VALUE of EPISODE-DURATION)
Help

> **Please enter the possible values of Time-Required.**
>
> (e.g., values for COST are: free, cheap, low, moderate, medium-high high not-insured)
>
> IMMEDIATE FEW-MINUTES AN-HOUR FEW-HOURS A-DAY FEW-DAYS WEEKS MONTHS

> **Is there an ordering over the possible values for Time-required?**
>
> Yes ✓
> No
> *Help*

> **Can there be more than one Time-required?**
>
> Yes
> No ✓
> *Help*

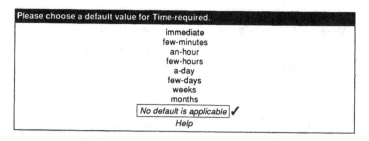

Please choose a default value for Time-required.
immediate
few-minutes
an-hour
few-hours
a-day
few-days
weeks
months
No default is applicable ✓
Help

Once the intentional properties of the feature are acquired, the values of the feature applied to the elements of its domain are elicited. For static attributes, ASK presents a table of the objects to which it applies, and the user specifies the value of the feature for each object. In the current example, the user enters the value of the time-required feature for all diagnostic tests, including the training examples EKG and Upper-GI-series. The table below shows the value of time-required for EKG, after it was entered by the user.

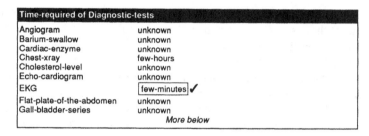

Time-required of Diagnostic-tests
Angiogram	unknown
Barium-swallow	unknown
Cardiac-enzyme	unknown
Chest-xray	few-hours
Cholesterol-level	unknown
Echo-cardiogram	unknown
EKG	few-minutes ✓
Flat-plate-of-the-abdomen	unknown
Gall-bladder-series	unknown

More below

4.7. Using the New Feature in Justifications

When the expert has finished defining time-required, the system can use it as any other feature and ASK can offer it as a possible justification. The dialog now returns to the justification interface, where the user selects the time-required as a justification for choosing EKG over Upper-GI-series:

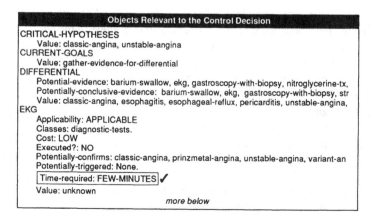

Objects Relevant to the Control Decision
CRITICAL-HYPOTHESES
    Value: classic-angina, unstable-angina
CURRENT-GOALS
    Value: gather-evidence-for-differential
DIFFERENTIAL
    Potential-evidence: barium-swallow, ekg, gastroscopy-with-biopsy, nitroglycerine-tx,
    Potentially-conclusive-evidence: barium-swallow, ekg, gastroscopy-with-biopsy, str
    Value: classic-angina, esophagitis, esophageal-reflux, pericarditis, unstable-angina,
EKG
    Applicability: APPLICABLE
    Classes: diagnostic-tests.
    Cost: LOW
    Executed?: NO
    Potentially-confirms: classic-angina, prinzmetal-angina, unstable-angina, variant-an
    Potentially-triggered: None.
    Time-required: FEW-MINUTES ✓
    Value: unknown
                        more below

Justifications for the Current Control Decision
GATHER-EVIDENCE-FOR-DIFFERENTIAL is in the CURRENT-GOALS. EKG is in the POTENTIAL-EVIDENCE of DIFFERENTIAL. UPPER-GI-SERIES is in the POTENTIAL-EVIDENCE of DIFFERENTIAL. *The COST of EKG is low.* *The TIME-REQUIRED of EKG is few-minutes.* *The TIME-REQUIRED of UPPER-GI-SERIES is a-day.*

At this point in the dialog, the user has indicated that the cost and time required of actions are factors to consider when choosing actions. The first three justifications represent the factors that the system would consider and were suggested by ASK. The user could have removed some of these seed justifications but did not in this case. From the combined set of justifications, ASK can generate a new strategy rule.

4.8. Generating and Generalizing a Strategy Rule

Given the user's justifications, ASK formulates a new strategy rule that accounts for the expert's critique of the system's performance. The new rule causes the expert's preferred action to be selected on the next iteration.

The left-hand side of the new rule is constructed by transforming the list of justifications into left-hand-side clauses. The transformation from justifications to rule clauses is fairly straightforward. The internal representation of justifications is very similar to the clause form of strategy rules. The right-hand-side recommendation (in this case, SELECT) was decided by the credit assignment analysis. In the current example, ASK forms the following rule:

```
IF   (IN gather-evidence-for-differential (current-goals))
     (IN ?ACTION (potential-evidence differential))
     (≤ (cost ?ACTION) low)
     (= (time-required ?ACTION) few-minutes)
THEN (SELECT ?ACTION)
```

In the process of forming rule clauses from justifications, ASK applies generalization operators. One operator is called *turning constants into variables.* In the strategy rule above, references to EKG have been replaced with the free variable ?ACTION, which is bound at runtime by the strategy-rule interpreter to each action that has been proposed and has not been filtered. The result is that the rule recommends the class of actions sharing the features of EKG in the justifications: the cost and time required.

Another generalization operator is *extending the reference* of a feature from a test of equality to a test over some range or set of permissible values. In the example strategy rule, the ≤ operator specifies that the third clause will succeed when the action has any value of cost equal to or less than low. ASK used a heuristic for applying this generalization; it found another selection rule that used ≤ for the cost feature.

In this example, however, ASK has no a priori information to help in extending the reference of the new feature, time-required. It asks the user for guidance by posing hypothetical variants on the current case to obtain boundary conditions on the acceptable range for the time-required clause in this rule. Since ASK lacks common sense, it has to ask whether the user would still accept the EKG if it takes no time at all:

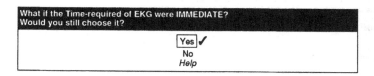

Then ASK offers near-miss cases:

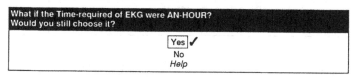

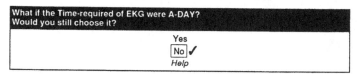

Given this information, ASK replaces the clause

```
(= (time-required ?ACTION) few-minutes)
```

with the clause

```
(≤ (time-required ?ACTION) few-hours).
```

4.9 Verifying a Rule

To evaluate the face validity of the generated rule, ASK presents a paraphrased translation to the user for verification. It also shows the operational consequences of the rule.

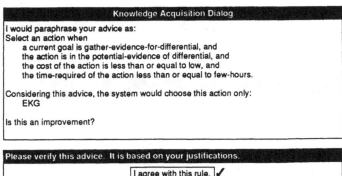

This completes one session of the knowledge acquisition dialog. With the new strategy rule, the performance system now recommends only the positive example, EKG, when the goal is to gather evidence and the actions are potentially diagnostic. The new selection rule fails to match the negative example and the other proposed actions, and it shadows the more general rule that formerly matched all seven actions.

The next subsection demonstrates how ASK can be used to acquire tradeoffs in a utility space. It is not essential to understanding the basic approach.

4.10. Acquiring Tradeoffs

The strategy rule just acquired is one of a family of rules that together constitute a strategy for selecting diagnostic actions. Selection rules can be viewed as tradeoffs among features, and a family of selection rules represents a set of acceptable tradeoffs. The new rule specifies that a moderate amount of time is acceptable if the cost is low and the diagnosticity is moderate.

In terms of utility theory, the new rule occupies a region in a space with dimensions defined by the features measuring diagnosticity, cost, and timeliness. Points in this space can be interpreted as the values of a multiattribute utility function [Keeney and Raiffa 1976]. The dimensions are attributes and the regions represent values of equivalent utility. The shadows relation among rules corresponds to a partial order over values of utility; some regions have higher utility than others in the same attribute space. For example, because of the shadows relation, the new rule takes precedence over selection rules that mention only cost or time-required. The region corresponding to the new rule can be interpreted as having higher utility. In other words, actions selected by the new rule are preferred over actions that would have been selected by shadowed rules.

To illustrate how ASK can be used to acquire other tradeoffs in the same space, this subsection sketches a second session where the user finds an exception to an existing rule.

In this second scenario, the user runs the performance system on a case where initial data provides evidence that the patient could have a very serious condition which requires immediate diagnosis. In this situation, the system suggests a set of actions that are potential evidence for hypotheses on the differential and have low cost. However, the user indicates that the system should ignore cost and concentrate on evidence that is potentially *conclusive* for hypotheses that are *critical*. The relevant objects and justification windows appear as follows:

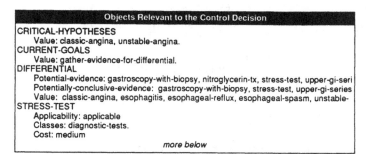

The positive example is Stress-test, which was not selected by the system because its cost was more than low. The negative example is Nitroglycerine-tx, which was selected by the system. The justifications in the window shown above were seeded by ASK; they correspond to the clauses of the strategy rules that picked Nitroglycerine-tx and not Stress-test.

In the justification session, the user tells ASK to consider *conclusive* evidence for *critical* hypotheses. The set of critical hypotheses is already represented by a knowledge-base object. Critical-hypotheses is defined as a set of hypotheses that are active (and therefore on the differential) and time-critical (a feature of hypotheses). The relationship between conclusive evidence and critical hypotheses is *not* currently represented by a feature. The relationship *is* currently defined for the set of hypotheses on the differential. Since the set of critical hypotheses and the differential share the same domain, the feature implementing the potentially-conclusive-evidence relationship can be applied to the critical-hypotheses object. The user accomplishes this by clicking on the critical-hypothesis object and performing the operations shown in the following windows.

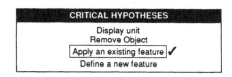

```
┌─────────────────────────────────────┐
│     Members of the class FEATURES    │
├─────────────────────────────────────┤
│              ACTIVE-P                │
│            APPLICABILITY             │
│              CLASSES                 │
│               COST                   │
│             CRITICALITY              │
│          DIAGNOSTIC-DATA             │
│             EXECUTED?                │
│           EXPECTED-COST              │
│            GENERALITY                │
│          LEVEL-OF-SUPPORT            │
│         NETWORK-DEPENDENTS           │
│          POTENTIAL-EVIDENCE          │
│ ┌─────────────────────────────────┐ │
│ │ POTENTIALLY-CONCLUSIVE-EVIDENCE │ │ ✔
│ └─────────────────────────────────┘ │
│         POTENTIALLY-RULES-OUT        │
│         POTENTIALLY-TRIGGERED        │
│           TIME-CRITICALITY           │
│            TRIGGER-LEVEL             │
│               VALUE                  │
└─────────────────────────────────────┘
```

The feature potentially-conclusive-evidence was conveniently defined to work for any set of hypotheses, and critical-hypotheses is a set of hypotheses. As a result, when the user applies the feature to critical-hypotheses, the set of potentially conclusive evidence for critical hypotheses is immediately computed. The newly-applied feature is displayed in the relevant objects window and becomes available as a justification. The updated relevant objects window shows the value of the feature as the singleton set containing the action Stress-test. In the window shown below the user selects this fact as a justification for choosing the stress test.

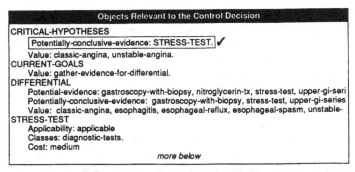

With this set of justifications, ASK generates the rule paraphrased to the user as follows:

```
Select an action when
    a current goal is gather-evidence-for-differential, and
    the action is in the potential-evidence of differential, and
    the action is in the potentially-confirming-evidence of critical-hypotheses, and
    the cost of the action is ignored.
```

The final clause of the rule is a positive form of the *dropping conditions* generalization operator. It specifies explicitly that the cost criterion, which was mentioned in the system's existing rule, should be overridden by this new rule. The ignore clauses are used in determining the shadowing relationship among strategy rules (Section 3.5). This new rule will shadow the existing rule. The operational effect is that the actions that are potentially conclusive for critical hypotheses will be selected regardless of cost, if there are any such actions and hypotheses; otherwise, actions that provide evidence for any active hypotheses and have low cost will be selected.

5. Experience Using ASK

This section reports briefly on some test sessions performed to evaluate ASK. More detailed analysis of these experiments and the positive and negative results may be found in [Gruber 1989].

ASK has been tested for the *prospective diagnosis* task [Cohen, Greenberg, and Delisio 1987] in the domain of chest pain, which is the problem addressed by the MUM system and used as an example performance system in this article. The original MUM strategy, the strategic phase planner described in [Cohen, et al. 1987], was written by a knowledge engineer as a set of knowledge sources implemented in Lisp. ASK was used by its designer to (re)acquire MUM's strategic knowledge from scratch in the form of strategy rules.

ASK was also tested with the physician who served as the domain expert for MUM. He was able to add domain-specific strategic knowledge to an existing general strategy in dialogs like those demonstrated in Section 4. In one session, the original domain expert taught a colleague how to use ASK. In general, this experience suggested that the following conditions are important for success at helping the domain expert teach a diagnostic strategy to ASK:

- The relevant control features are defined in advance (e.g., potentially-conclusive-evidence relation of Section 4.10) or are analogous to existing features (e.g., the definition of time-required, which is analogous to cost, can be elicited by example as shown in Section 4.6). When new features have no analog, then it may require knowledge engineering skills to define them. The problem of defining features is discussed in Section 6.3.
- The user understands the opportunistic control model that underlies the strategy-rule representation. If the user does not understand how the strategic knowledge is used, he or she may not give ASK useful information upon which to build strategy rules. For example, when the second physician used ASK for the first time, he tried to get it to follow a procedure-like plan: e.g., ask *all* the history and examination questions before proposing *any* diagnostic tests. This caused ASK to construct an overly general strategy rule, as described in Section 6.3.

Some representational limitations of the strategy-rule approach to control were revealed in another experiment in which ASK was used to reimplement NEOMYCIN's diagnostic strategy. One difference between ASK's strategy rules and NEOMYCIN's tasks and metarules [Clancey 1988; Clancey and Bock 1988] is the way in which the problem-solving state is represented. In NEOMYCIN, metarules are invoked by tasks, and tasks are invoked like subroutines with arguments. Some of the problem-solving state is represented by the calling stack for task invocation. In addition, metarules access and set global variables. These computational properties make certain kinds of strategic knowledge easier to represent. The task structure serves as a natural representation for goal-directed control, and the global variables and task arguments encourage a strategy with a persistent focus on the "current hypothesis" and "current finding." In contrast, ASK's strategy rules have no hierarchical calling structure and cannot set global variables. As a consequence, it is difficult to implement a goal-directed (top-down) strategy or to manipulate the differential as a data structure. ASK's representation and the corresponding elicitation metaphor is more suited to acquiring an opportunistic strategy.

In principle, one can completely reproduce the observable behavior of the NEOMYCIN strategy using ASK, because the strategy-rule language together with MU's control features are Turing complete. In practice, knowledge engineering skills were required to coerce the desired behavior from strategy rules, mainly by defining control features. For example, the engineer using ASK had to define special control features to correspond to NEOMYCIN's "current hypothesis" and "pursued hypothesis" which were stated more naturally with metarules and variables in the NEOMYCIN language. The engineering effort went into defining sophisticated features. ASK is more helpful for building up associations between existing features and actions in strategic decisions.

6. Analysis: Scope of Applicability, Assumptions, and Limitations

Although the approach taken with ASK is independent of any domain, it necessarily sacrifices generality for power. The ASK approach commits to a method of applying strategic knowledge that iteratively chooses among individual actions, employs strategy rules for the representation, and bases new knowledge on justifications of choices of actions. As a consequence, ASK has limited scope and requires some strong assumptions. This section will characterize the scope of applicability of ASK in terms of properties of a class of performances tasks and will explicate the critical assumptions and limitations that are inherent in the approach.

6.1. Characteristics of Tasks to Which ASK Applies

The problems to which ASK can be applied are those for which expert strategy is essential to the performance task and for which the strategy-rule knowledge representation and MU architecture are adequate. This is not a circular definition; it states that the applicability of the acquisition tool depends largely on the adequacy of the performance representation. Representational adequacy is judged with respect to the class of performance tasks and the problem-solving method for which a representation is designed (see Section 2.1). So, ASK's applicability will be characterized in terms of tasks for which the strategy-rule representation and the strategy-rule control cycle are appropriate.

The major characteristics of tasks to which ASK would apply are as follows:

Actions can be selected one at a time (as opposed to sequences of action). A task for which this characteristic often holds is reactive planning for robots, where uncertainty about the world and real-time constraints necessitate acting without projection. Robots controlled by reactive planners select actions on the basis of immediate features of the environment, without projecting the consequences of several possible sequences of actions and picking the best sequence.

A task for which selecting actions one at a time is *not* appropriate is planning a set of drugs to cover an infection. MYCIN's therapy algorithm, for example, selects a collection of drugs to cover a set of infectious organisms using an algorithm written in Lisp [Clancey 1984]. This task necessitates reasoning about the *collective* properties of groups of drugs and organisms. Since the utility of individual actions depends strongly on the other actions to be selected at the same time, the strategy-rule representation could not capture the desired drug-selection expertise. (If every possible collection of drugs was represented as a "superaction," then strategy rules could represent drug-selection criteria. However, this is not feasible for large numbers of drugs, and it reduces all strategic reasoning to a single decision.)

Actions can be related directly to the situations in which they should be chosen. A positive example of a task with this property is selecting legal cases for argument, where cases are treated as actions. The merits of each case can be represented with features that describe its individual properties and its relationships to other cases and the current fact situation (e.g., Ashley's [1989] *dimensions*). A case-selection strategy might be modeled by relating the relevant features of legal situations to the features of cases that may be cited in the specified situations. For instance, in a trade secrets situation one might cite cases that make a claim about whether and how secrets were disclosed.

A negative example is the management of cancer treatment plans, the domain of the performance system ONCOCIN [Tu, et al. 1989]. The strategy for cancer treatment in ONCOCIN is represented with *protocols*: skeletal plans that are instantiated with therapeutic actions for particular patients. In attempting to model the individual treatment steps as actions in ASK, we found that the justifications for choosing the next action in cancer protocols were often statements of the form "because drug V is a member of the drug combination VAM, which is the next chemotherapy to be administered to this patient according to protocol 20-83-1" rather than "VAM is useful for small cell lung cancer because this combination can help prevent the tumor becoming resistant." The justifications also did not include a description of the context in which drugs V, A, and M are competing with other possible drugs. The knowledge underlying the recommendation of the VAM drug combination is compiled into the skeletal plan for a protocol. In this domain it is unrealistic to expect the experts to justify treatment plans with underlying reasons for their use, because by their very nature protocols are experiments designed to *test* the effectiveness of treatment strategies.

In general, the opportunistic style of control afforded by ASK's representation *generates* plans based on underlying reasons for taking plan steps (actions), when they are available. A memory-based planner unfolds and *instantiates* stored plans, in which individual actions need no independent justification. Applications requiring domain-specific strategic knowledge often do both styles of reasoning about action. *Within* an ONCOCIN protocol, for example, actions may be modified or dropped for reasons relating to the dynamic situation (e.g., the condition of the patient). Strategic knowledge for modifying steps within a plan could be formulated in strategy rules and acquired with ASK if the position of an action in a plan were abstracted as a control feature. In ONCOCIN this knowledge is, in fact, represented with rules that are indexed by protocols.[3]

Local action-selection criteria can avoid global pitfalls.   Computer players of adversarial games often are based on static evaluation of position. Their strategy for selecting a next move is to choose the action that scores best on the evaluation function. If the evaluation function can be structured as a conjunctive expression over features, ASK could be used to acquire it. For example, ASK can acquire the kind of strategy learned by Waterman's poker player: mappings from descriptions of the board and the opponent to betting actions [Waterman 1970]. A game-playing strategy based on mappings from features of game situations to classes of moves will succeed if the features are usefully predictive—if what looks good locally does not lead to global pitfalls.

A borderline negative example is chess, where strategy is often played out over several moves, and evaluation functions are prone to horizon effects. If the right features can be found, strategy rules can map them to actions and ASK can acquire them. If the features invented by the user lead to pitfalls, then acquiring rules that use these features will not produce a globally optimal strategy.

In general, strategy rules support the reactive style of reasoning, where features are immediately available. In contrast, search-based planning can explore the outcomes of actions into the simulated future and back up the evaluation of the utility of the results. Therefore, ASK can be useful for tasks in which the effects of actions cannot be accurately predicted. The features acquired by ASK combine predictions of effects and the expected utility of effects.

An optimal decision among actions is not required or possible for every choice of actions. The chest pain application is both a positive and negative example. Most of the evidence-gathering questions, tests, and therapies are chosen with relatively simple measures of utility, such as qualitative measures of diagnosticity, efficacy, and cost. In practice, the data and necessity to elicit probabilities and numeric estimates of utility for every possible combination of actions is not present. However, a negative example in the same domain is the *last* strategic decision that is typically made (or avoided): deciding whether to perform angiography and consequently open heart surgery. This decision has been successfully modeled using the techniques of decision analysis [Pauker and Kassirer 1981].

There is no reason in principle why ASK's model of selecting actions cannot be described in terms of expected utility, nor is there any fundamental reason why a Bayesian utility function could not be used as a feature in strategy rules. The practical difference is in how a utility model is constructed. A set of strategy rules form a qualitative model of the utility of actions, where the union of actions recommended by rules are treated as equivalent. A multiattribute decision model [Keeney and Raiffa 1976] makes finer-grained, numeric estimates of the relative utility of each attribute, and combines them to rank the recommended actions.

6.2. Critical Assumptions

ASK makes progress in automating the acquisition of strategic knowledge, but many aspects of this difficult problem are not solved. What is left for further work is revealed by the assumptions that the ASK approach makes about the available knowledge and the people that can provide it. Some key assumptions are discussed here, and a more complete list is supplied in [Gruber 1989].

Requirements on the substantive knowledge. The ASK approach assumes that substantive knowledge of the performance system: 1) is already acquired or can be acquired, 2) is correct, and 3) is sufficient for making the distinctions necessary for the strategic knowledge.

The control features used by ASK depend on existing substantive knowledge in the inference network of a MU performance system. For example, in diagnostic tasks, much of the important substantive knowledge is found in combination functions which specify how evidential support values and other inferential values are propagated through the inference network. In the MU environment, combination functions are acquired with a symbol-level interface—editors that present and elicit knowledge in the same form as it is used (i.e., rules, slot values, etc.). ASK assumes that the MU interface is adequate for acquiring substantive knowledge.

A more serious problem is the assumption that the substantive knowledge is correct. ASK's credit assignment algorithm determines what type of rule to acquire and which objects the rule must match and not match. The algorithm is based on the assumption that the features mentioned in existing strategy rules are correct. To account for the discrepancy between system and user actions, a new rule must match different features or different values of features than the existing strategy rules. If the features return incorrect values for some actions, this algorithm cannot correctly attribute the blame.

Finally, ASK assumes that the features that are already defined or are easily defined within the existing knowledge base are sufficient for representing the desired strategy. The experiment in reimplementing NEOMYCIN described in Section 5 was an opportunity to test this assumption. NEOMYCIN's strategy makes heavy use of the subsumption relation among hypotheses. For example, one metarule specifies that, "If the hypothesis being focused upon has a child that has not been pursued, then pursue that child." The CHILD metarelation assumed by this rule is a subsumption relation among hypotheses that was not present in the MUM knowledge base used in our experiment. It was simply not possible to acquire this strategic knowledge without reorganizing the substantive knowledge base (i.e., identifying abstract categories of diseases and relating them in a hierarchy to the existing diseases).

In general, the overall effectiveness of ASK in acquiring strategic knowledge is bounded by the difficulty of representing the relevant control features for the domain.

Validity of experts' justifications for acquiring strategy.   It was argued in Section 1 that the acquisition of strategic knowledge is difficult because domain experts do not normally express their strategy in a form that is generative, operational, and general (i.e., because of representation mismatch). However, it is observed that experts *can* give justifications for specific strategic decisions. The approach taken in ASK requires a strong assumption: that experts' justifications form a valid basis for acquiring the strategic knowledge of systems. There are several ways that this assumption might be wrong.

One way is the problem of tacit knowledge—that the knowledge we wish to acquire from experts is not explicitly present in what they tell us. An influential theory in cognitive science argues that the knowledge underlying expertise is often tacit due to the process of *knowledge compilation* [Anderson 1986]. As experts learn problem-solving strategies from experience in a domain, they internalize the useful associations between situations and actions and become unaware of the inferential steps that they may have made as novices. For example, physicians in an educational setting may teach diagnostic strategy one way and practice it another way. In experimental settings, when people are asked to account for their decisions retrospectively they often refer to causal theories or judgments of plausibility rather than the pertinent stimuli and their responses [Nisbett and Wilson 1977]. And some writers argue that the difference between being able to act and being able to talk about action is fundamental—that computer models of action are essentially incapable of capturing the real basis for action [Winograd and Flores 1986].

If experts cannot account for their strategic decisions, ASK cannot acquire the strategic expertise in a program. There is a difference, however, between assuming that experts can describe their own cognitive processes and assuming that they can justify their behavior. ASK only depends on the latter assumption. The assumptions that experts can provide valid justifications may be reformulated as the requirement that experts be good teachers. Remember that ASK is designed to acquire knowledge for choosing actions that are observable and, therefore, objectively justifiable. The fact that medical school professors may not practice what they preach does not mean that the justifications are invalid. On the contrary, good teachers can account for behavior in a principled way and in objective terms, even though their compiled expertise may not follow from their explanations.

A second problem with the reliance on expert-supplied justifications is the assumption that domain experts can invent useful abstractions of the domain—the right control features. In the same way that an autonomous machine-learning program is limited by the description language provided by the program author, a knowledge acquisition system such as ASK is dependent on the abstraction skills of the user.[4] ASK relies on the user to invent features that not only are sufficient to distinguish actions in specific cases, but also lay out a space of relevant generalizations. This assumption would be unfounded if the expert defined a unique feature for every training case; the resulting strategy—a lookup table of special cases— would be brittle. It is also possible that an expert can describe useful features in natural language but cannot implement them.

The validity of an assumption about the skill level of users is an empirical question, and the answers will depend on the subjects and the tasks. ASK helps frame the research question by distinguishing between the ability to *invent* the necessary features, which is structured by the elicitation of justifications, and the *implementation* of features, which is partially supported by a symbol-level interface for defining features. If an ASK user cannot implement a feature but knows what it should represent, she calls the knowledge engineer. The acquisition of features (new terms) is an interesting area for further study.

6.3. Major Limitations

Two of the fundamental limitations to the approach taken in ASK are discussed in this section. A more complete analysis is given in [Gruber 1989].

6.3.1. Reliance on Knowledge Engineering Skills   It should be clear from the preceding discussion that ASK depends on the ability of the user to define and implement control features. The fact that many features are not easy to implement means that ASK is still limited by the operationalization aspect of representation mismatch. The problem of operationalizing terms is relevant to any learning system whose description language can be extended by the user. Although ASK provides a helpful interface for defining new features, some new features require programming to implement. The problem is not a matter of learning the notation; one needs to know a lot more than the syntax of Lisp to be able to implement control features that capture sophisticated assessments of the state of problem solving. To implement a feature such as the potentially conclusive-evidence relation, one needs to understand the workings of the MU architecture at the symbol level. That is the expertise of knowledge engineers, not domain experts.

There is a way in which ASK's elicitation technique can actually aggravate the problem of representation mismatch. ASK is designed to present the "user illusion" [Kay 1984] of an interface that accepts *explanations* for strategic decisions. In contrast, a symbol-level acquisition tool such as TEIRESIAS [Davis 1976] supports a straightforward interface to rules without disguising them as anything else. The problem with a system such as ASK that presents a knowledge-level interface to the user but internally makes symbol-level distinctions is that the user's model of how the system works can differ significantly from how the system actually functions. If the user's model is inaccurate, she cannot predict what the system will do with what is elicited. The result is a breakdown in communication and a failure in the knowledge acquisition process.

One of the experiments in which ASK was used by physicians illustrates a case in which the user's ignorance of the operational semantics of strategy rules resulted in an unintended strategy. The expert wanted to teach the system to ask all applicable questions of one class before asking any applicable questions of another. He answered ASK's prompts in such a way that the credit assignment algorithm determined that it needed to acquire a filter rule, when in fact a selection rule was needed. When the expert explained (with justifications) that questions of one type should *not* be selected, ASK generated a filter rule that prohibited questions of that type from *ever* being selected, which is a gross overgeneralization. The error was not apparent until the actions from the first class were exhausted and the system could not suggest any more actions to perform. To have avoided this problem, the user would have had to understand the operational difference between filter and selection rules and the correspondence between his answers to ASK's prompts and the type of rule being acquired.

6.3.2. Overgeneralization Due to the Lack of a Training Set   Although ASK uses generalization operators, it differs from most inductive learning techniques in that it does not learn from a large training set of examples. The user is responsible for choosing training examples that will produce useful generalizations. Unfortunately, the lack of a large training set limits the extent to which ASK can help with the generalization problem.

It is easy to generate strategy rules with ASK that are overly general, because of the elicitation technique. Adding justifications specializes the resulting strategy rule; doing nothing leaves it general. Consider two strategic situations in the medical workup. In the early phase, actions are selected for their low cost and minimal diagnosticity. In later phases, actions that offer a potentially significant diagnostic or therapeutic value are selected at higher cost, even if lower-cost actions are available. If the selection rules for the first phase were acquired without any clauses identifying the strategic situation (i.e., features of the early phase), then the rules acquired for the early phase would also match when the later phase arose. There is no knowledge-free way for ASK to anticipate the missing clauses that specify the context in which a rule should apply.

In practice, overgeneralizations of this type are discouraged by starting with an initial set of strategy rules that specify the basic strategic situations to distinguish. These rules serve as the basis for seed justifications (Section 4.5) upon which the user builds a set of justifications for a specific case. The knowledge engineer can provide a set of very general strategy rules, anticipating some of the situations in which domain-specific tradeoffs will arise. Then the major role of the user is to *specialize* the general strategy with application-specific strategic knowledge. Overgeneralizations are still likely, however, when the user fails to elaborate the features of a novel context in which a selection is made among specific actions.

If ASK kept a library of training cases, it might be able to check newly formed rules for inconsistency with past training and prevent excessive overgeneralization. Each case in a library would need the values of all relevant features of the positive and negative examples and the features specifying the strategic situation. When a new rule is proposed, it could be tested against the objects in the case. If the new rule recommended a different outcome than the stored case, and did not shadow the rule associated with the case, then the two rules would be inconsistent. Unfortunately, keeping a library of cases is not trivial because the space of features can grow with experience. If a new rule mentions a new feature, it is incomparable with previous cases that did not mention the feature, unless the feature is static (i.e., its value does not change during the execution of the performance system). A general solution is to store a snapshot of the entire working memory with each case, so that all possible relevant features could be derived. This solution could be expensive. The whole issue of how to store experience for future learning is an intriguing avenue for research. Some promising approaches have been developed for case-based learning systems [e.g., Bareiss 1989; Hammond 1989].

7. Discussion: Key Design Decisions

Design decisions are often hidden sources of power in AI systems. This section discusses a few characteristics of ASK's design as they relate to its function as an automated knowledge acquisition tool.

The strategy-rule representation supported by ASK is neither a novel way of formulating strategy nor an ad hoc design. For the purpose of *implementing* strategic knowledge, a procedural representation such as a Lisp function or an augmented transition network would have been more flexible. The goals in designing a representation for ASK are to be able to capture strategic knowledge in an executable form *and* to be able to elicit it from experts.

Strategy rules were designed to represent mappings between states of the inference network and equivalence classes of actions, for each of three operations: propose, filter, and select. The declarative clausal form of strategy rules allows for execution by conventional unification-style matching and corresponds to the structure of justifications. Limiting the operational effects of rules to propose, filter, and select operations simplifies credit assignment and conflict resolution. The result is a representation in which strategic knowledge can be acquired.

Two of the design decisions that led to this representation are critical to ASK's techniques for automated knowledge acquisition. First, strategic knowledge has been formulated as classification knowledge. Second, a global strategy is represented as a family of strategy rules with fine-grained effects. The rationale for each decision is given below.

7.1. Formulating Strategic Knowledge as Classification Knowledge

Strategy rules structure knowledge about what to do next as knowledge for classification: associations between strategic situations and classes of actions. The following capabilities follow from this design.

The ability to use conventional machine learning techniques. ASK can use simple syntactic induction operators for generalization (turning constants into variables, dropping conditions, and extending reference). Whereas the problem of learning sequences and procedures with internal states is very hard [Dietterich and Michalski 1986], the problem of learning classification rules is well understood [Dietterich and Michalski 1983]. If mappings from states to actions define the classes of state descriptions in which actions are appropriate, a learner can generalize control knowledge by generalizing class descriptions.

The ability to elicit machine-understandable information at the knowledge level. ASK can elicit applicability conditions for control decisions in machine-understandable terms, because the justifications from the user's point of view correspond to clauses in the rule representation. The list of justifications can be elicited in any order, since they are used as conjuncts in the class descriptions.

The ability to use simple explanations for input and output. ASK can use simple template-based natural language generation to provide explanations. ASK's explanations are just lists of facts relevant to the current control decision paraphrased in English; they are essentially the same as justifications. ASK can get away with this simple explanation technique because every control decision is a flat match of situations and associated actions. Because there is no implicit state, such as there is in an evolving control plan, the context of the decision to choose an action is fully explained by the clauses of matching strategy rules. The English explanation—paraphrases of instantiated clauses—corresponds to what is happening at the symbol level.[5]

The use of explicit, abstract control knowledge for explanation was developed in the work of Swartout, et al. [Swartout 1983; Neches, Swartout, and Moore 1985] and Clancey [Clancey 1983a, 1983b]. ASK follows the principle arising from their work that an explanation of surface behavior should correspond to the structure of the system's strategy. However, in contrast to serious attempts at knowledge-system explanation, ASK's explanations do not describe the goal structure and focusing behavior of the system because the performance architecture does not support the corresponding control mechanisms (e.g., goal stacks, tasks, etc.).

The inability to acquire goal-directed plans.   As a consequence of formulating strategy as simple classification, it is awkward to acquire goal-directed strategy with ASK. To capture the knowledge for reasoning about action at different abstraction levels, the strategy-rule representation would have to be extended to support hierarchical planning in the sense of ABSTRIPS [Sacerdoti 1974]. Currently, all strategy rules within each category (propose, filter, select) are matched in parallel at each iteration. In one extension proposed in [Gruber 1989], the rules would be partitioned into abstraction levels; at each level, rules would choose the subgoals for the lower abstraction level until the subgoals at the lowest level are grounded in individual actions. It is not clear whether the added structure would compromise the comprehensibility of the elicitation technique; this is a question for future research.

7.2. Formulating Strategy as Fine-Grained Reactions

Recall the third aspect of representation mismatch: domain experts have more difficulty devising a general procedure that accounts for their strategic expertise than describing what they actually do in specific cases. ASK shows that strategic knowledge can be acquired from experts if it is elicited in the context of specific choices among actions and then generalized. This is possible because strategy rules model local decisions about actions that can be generalized to classes of situations and actions. In theory, what appears to be a global strategy can emerge from a series of local strategic decisions. For example, Chapman and Agre [1986] propose that complex, coherent behavior arises from the continued activation of situation-action structures without top-down control.

There is empirical support for the notion that globally coherent plans can be acquired by eliciting the knowledge for local decisions. For example, SALT succeeds at acquiring knowledge about how to construct globally satisfactory solutions to a class of design problems [Marcus 1987, 1988]. SALT elicits from designers knowledge about constraints among individual parts—information that is relatively easy to specify—and offers help for putting the pieces together. SALT's results are relevant to ASK because constructing a solution requires managing the *process* by which parts are assembled under constraints; this is similar to managing the selection of actions. SALT can acquire the requisite knowledge from experts because it decomposes the larger task of assembling a solution into small decisions about what part to add, how to (immediately) check it for constraints, and how to recover from those violated constraints.

One can view SALT's design task and ASK's action-selection task as varieties of planning, where configured parts and diagnostic actions correspond to plan steps. This view reveals an important difference between the two architectures. SALT's planning method provides for a backtracking search, whereas ASK's planning method is purely reactive, with no projection (lookahead) and no possibility to undo actions. This may prove to be an important variable in the question of whether knowledge of local decisions can add up to a global strategy.

8. Conclusion

The immediate outcome of this research is a method for partially automating the acquisition of strategic knowledge from experts. The issues that are raised, however, are more significant than the ASK program itself. Strategic knowledge was chosen for the study of knowledge acquisition because it illuminates the problems of representation mismatch. Furthermore, an extreme solution was selected—a declarative representation of reactive control knowledge—to test conjectures about sources of power for knowledge acquisition. The results have been analyzed in the preceding discussions of the scope of applicability, assumptions, limitations, and design decisions. This section concludes with a more general point brought out by this work and the future research it suggests.

If representation mismatch describes the problem of knowledge acquisition, then solutions should offer some way to bridge the representational gap between the domain expert and the implementation. This suggests that the design of knowledge representations is central to addressing the knowledge acquisition problem. This article has emphasized the motivations for and implications of ASK's representation of strategic knowledge in an effort to elucidate principles of *design for acquisition*: how to design knowledge systems to facilitate the acquisition of the knowledge they need.

Earlier reports [Bylander and Chandrasekaran 1987; Gruber and Cohen 1987] describe how knowledge representations and methods for task-level architectures can facilitate *manual* knowledge acquisition (i.e., mediated by tools that are passive). The design of representations can reduce representation mismatch from the implementation side by providing (generic) task-level primitives which enable experts to work directly with the knowledge base.

The ASK research illustrates how *automated* knowledge acquisition can help overcome representation mismatch by eliciting knowledge in a form that is available from experts and yet is very close to an operational, generalizable representation. Again, the design of representations plays a central role in the success of the knowledge acquisition process. The major contributions of ASK to the process—active elicitation of justifications, credit assignment, and syntactic generalization—are enabled by the declarative, role-restricted rule representation. At the same time, the kind of strategic knowledge that can be acquired— opportunistic and reactive rather than goal-directed and plan-driven—is a function of what can be naturally represented in strategy rules.

A similar power/generality tradeoff can be found in most knowledge acquisition tools. At the power end of the continuum lie OPAL-class elicitation tools [Freiling and Alexander 1984; Gale 1987; Musen, et al. 1987], which acquire knowledge in representations customized to a problem-solving method and a particular domain. OPAL employs elicitation techniques that are customized for both the skeletal-plan refinement method used in ONCOCIN and the domain of cancer therapy. As a result, OPAL can be used by domain experts. At the generality end lie TEIRESIAS-class tools [Davis 1976; Boose and Bradshaw 1987; Shachter and Heckerman 1987], which acquire knowledge at the symbol-level for formalisms that are not committed to particular tasks or domains. TEIRESIAS makes it easy to enter and modify rules but requires the user to bridge the representational gap from the domain- and problem-specific description to the backward-chaining architecture. Somewhere in the middle are the MOLE-class tools [Eshelman 1988; Klinker 1988; Marcus 1988], which acquire knowledge in representations that are method-specific and domain-independent. This article has shown several ways in which the design of ASK trades the generality of a representation useful for knowledge engineering for the power of a restricted representation suitable for automated knowledge acquisition.

Further research is needed to investigate how knowledge representations and reasoning methods can be designed to make the task of knowledge acquisition more amenable to computer-assisted techniques for elicitation and learning.

Acknowledgments

This article reports on the author's doctoral research directed by Paul Cohen at the University of Massachusetts, Department of Computer and Information Science. The work was supported by DARPA-RADC contract F30602-85-C0014 and ONR University Research Initiative contract N00014-86-K-1764. The paper was written at the Stanford Knowledge Systems Laboratory with funding from Tektronics, Inc. Computing facilities were provided by the SUMEX-AIM resource under NIH grant RR-00785.

Discussions with many colleagues have contributed to the ideas in this paper, including Kevin Ashley, Jim Bennett, B. Chandrasekaran, Bill Clancey, David Day, Larry Fagan, Richard Fikes, Michael Freiling, Victor Lesser, John McDermott, Mark Musen, Paul Utgoff, and especially Paul Cohen. I am very grateful to Ray Bareiss, Tilda Brown, Paul Cohen, Richard Keller, Sandra Marcus, Mark Musen, Bruce Porter, and Nancy Wogrin for thoughtful and careful reviews of earlier drafts of this paper.

Notes

1. Dietterich and Bennett [1988] refer to "making goals achievable" and "making goals more useful."
2. Control features correspond to the *metarelations* in Clancey's tasks-and-metarules representation [Clancey and Bock 1988].
3. Thanks to Lawrence Fagan, Mark Musen, and Samson Tu for their help with this analysis.
4. Getting the right primitive features has always been essential to getting a machine learning program to find useful generalizations. For example, Quinlan [1983] reports having spent three months devising a good set of attributes (board position features for chess) so that the learning program ID3 could produce a decision tree in seconds.
5. This is an oversimplification. In actuality, the shadowing relations among strategy rules are not reflected in the explanation. Not surprisingly, they are a source of confusion for users, possibly because they do not fit the simple conceptual model of situation–action.

References

Agre, P.E., and Chapman, D. 1987. Pengi: An implementation of a theory of activity. *Proceedings of the Sixth National Conference on Artificial Intelligence* (pp. 268–272). Seattle, Washington: Morgan Kaufmann.

Anderson, J.R. 1986. Knowledge compilation: the general learning mechanism. In R.S. Michalski, J.G. Carbonell, and T.M. Mitchell (Eds.), *Machine learning: An artificial intelligence approach*, (Vol. 2). San Mateo, CA: Morgan Kaufmann.

Ashley, K.D. 1989. *Modelling legal argument: Reasoning with cases and hypotheticals*. Cambridge, MA: MIT Press. Based on doctoral dissertation, Department of Computer and Information Science, University of Massachusetts, Amherst.

Bareiss, E.R. 1989. *Exemplar-based knowledge acquisition: A unified approach to concept representation, classification, and learning*. Boston: Academic Press. Based on doctoral dissertation, Department of Computer Science, University of Texas, Austin.

Benjamin, D.P. 1987. Learning strategies by reasoning about rules. *Proceedings of the Tenth International Joint Conference on Artificial Intelligence* (pp. 256–259). Milan, Italy: Morgan Kaufmann.

Bennett, J.S. 1985. ROGET: A knowledge-based system for acquiring the conceptual structure of a diagnostic expert system. *Journal of Automated Reasoning, 1*, 49–74.

Boose, J.H. 1986. *Expertise Transfer for Expert System Design*. New York: Elsevier.

Boose, J.H., and Bradshaw, J.M. 1987. Expertise transfer and complex problems: Using AQUINAS as a knowledge acquisition workbench for expert systems. *International Journal of Man-Machine Studies, 26*, 21–25.

Buchanan, B.G., Barstow, D.K., Bechtel, R., Bennett, J., Clancey, W., Kulikowski, C., Mitchell, T., and Waterman, D.A. 1983. Constructing an expert system. In F. Hayes-Roth, D.A. Waterman, and D.B. Lenat (Eds.), *Building expert systems*. Reading, MA: Addison-Wesley.

Buchanan, B.G., and Shortliffe, E.H. 1984. *Rule-Based Expert Systems: The MYCIN Experiments of the Stanford Heuristic Programming Project*. Reading, MA: Addison-Wesley.

Bylander, R., and Chandrasekaran, B. 1987. Generic tasks for knowledge-based reasoning: The "right" level of abstraction for knowledge acquisition. *International Journal of Man-Machine Studies, 26*, 231–244.

Chandrasekaran, B. 1983. Toward a taxonomy of problem-solving types. *AI Magazine, 4*, 9–17.

Chandrasekaran, B. 1986. Generic tasks in knowledge-based reasoning: High-level building blocks for expert system design. *IEEE Expert, 1*, 23–30.

Chandrasekaran, B. 1987. Towards a functional architecture for intelligence based on generic information processing tasks. *Proceedings of the Tenth International Joint Conference on Artificial Intelligence* (pp. 1183–1192). Milan, Italy: Morgan Kaufmann.

Chapman, D., and Agre, P.E. 1987. Abstract reasoning as emergent from concrete activity. In M.P. Georgeff and A.L. Lansky (Eds.), *Reasoning About Actions and Plans, Proceedings of the 1986 Workshop at Timberline, Oregon* (pp. 411–424).

Clancey, W.J. 1983a. The epistemology of a rule-based expert system—A framework for explanation. *Artificial Intelligence, 20*, 215–251.

Clancey, W.J. 1983b. The advantages of abstract control knowledge in expert system design. *Proceedings of the Third National Conference on Artificial Intelligence* (pp. 74–78). Washington, D.C.: Morgan Kaufmann.

Clancey, W.J. 1984. Details of the revised therapy algorithm. In B.G. Buchanan and E.H. Shortliffe (Eds.), *Rule-based expert systems: The MYCIN experiments of the Stanford Heuristic Programming Project*. Reading, MA: Addison-Wesley.

Clancey, W.J. 1985. Heuristic classification. *Artificial Intelligence, 27*, 289–350.

Clancey, W.J. 1988. Acquiring, representing, and evaluating a competence model of diagnosis. In Chi, Glaser, and Farr (Eds.), *Contributions to the nature of expertise* (pp. 343–418). Hillsdale, N.J.: Lawrence Erlbaum. Previously published as KSL Memo 84-2, Stanford University, February, 1984.

Clancey, W.J. 1989. Viewing knowledge bases as qualitative models. *IEEE Expert, 4*, 9–23. Previously published as Technical Report KSL-86-27, Stanford University.

Clancey, W.J., and Bock, C. 1988. Representing control knowledge as abstract tasks and metarules. In L. Bolc and M. Coombs (Eds.), *Expert system applications* (pp. 1–77). New York: Springer-Verlag.

Cohen, P.R., Day, D.S., Delisio, J., Greenberg, M., Kjeldsen, R., Suthers, D., and Berman, P. 1987. Management of uncertainty in medicine. *International Journal of Approximate Reasoning, 1*, 103–116.

Cohen, P.R., Greenberg, M., and Delisio, J. 1987. MU: A development environment for prospective reasoning systems. *Proceedings of the Sixth National Conference on Artificial Intelligence* (pp. 783–788). Seattle, Washington: Morgan Kaufmann.

Davis, R. 1976. *Applications of meta-level knowledge to the construction, maintenance, and use of large knowledge bases.* Doctoral dissertation, Computer Science Department, Stanford University. Reprinted in R. Davis and D.B. Lenat (Eds.), *Knowledge-based systems in artificial intelligence.* New York: McGraw-Hill, 1982.

DeJong, G., and Mooney, R.J. 1986. Explanation-based learning: An alternative view. *Machine Learning, 1,* 145–176.

Dietterich, T.G., and Bennett, J.S. 1988. Varieties of operationality. (Technical Report). Department of Computer Science, Oregon State University.

Dietterich. T.G., London, B., Clarkson, K., and Dromey, G. 1982. Learning and inductive inference. In P.R. Cohen and E. Feigenbaum (Eds.), *The handbook of artificial intelligence (Vol. 3).* Menlo Park, CA: Addison-Wesley.

Dietterich, T.G., and Michalski, R.S. 1983. A comparative review of selected methods for learning from examples. In R.S. Michalski, J.G. Carbonell, and T.M. Mitchell (Eds.), *Machine learning: An artificial intelligence approach.* San Mateo, CA: Morgan Kaufmann.

Dietterich, T.G., and Michalski, R.S. 1986. Learning to predict sequences. In R. Michalski, J. Carbonell, and T. Mitchell (Eds.), *Machine learning: An artificial intelligence approach (Vol. 2).* San Mateo, CA: Morgan Kaufmann.

Erman, L.D., Scott, A.C., and London, P.E. 1984. Separating and integrating control in a rule-based tool. *Proceedings of the IEEE Workshop of Knowledge-base Systems* (pp. 37–43). Denver, Colorado.

Eshelman, L. 1988. MOLE: A knowledge-acquisition tool for cover-and-differentiate systems. In S. Marcus (Ed.), *Automating knowledge acquisition for expert systems.* Boston: Kluwer Academic Publishers.

Firby, R.J. 1987. An investigation into reactive planning in complex domains. *Proceedings of the Sixth National Conference on Artificial Intelligence* (pp. 202–206). Seattle, Washington: Morgan Kaufmann.

Freiling, M.J., and Alexander, J.H. 1984. Diagrams and grammars: Tools for mass producing expert systems. *Proceedings of the First Conference on Artificial Intelligence Applications* (pp. 537–543). Denver, Colorado: IEEE Computer Society Press.

Friedland, P.E., and Iwasaki, Y. 1985. The concept and implementation of skeletal plans. *Journal of Automated Reasoning, 1,* 161–208.

Gale, W.A. 1987. Knowledge-based knowledge acquisition for a statistical consulting system. *International Journal of Man-Machine Studies, 13,* 81–116.

Golding, A., Rosenbloom, P.S., and Laird, J.E. 1987. Learning general search control from outside guidance. *Proceedings of the Tenth International Joint Conference on Artificial Intelligence* (pp. 334–337). Milan, Italy: Morgan Kaufmann.

Gruber, T.R. 1989. *The Acquisition of Strategic Knowledge.* Boston: Academic Press. Based on doctoral dissertation, Department of Computer and Information Science, University of Massachusetts.

Gruber, T.R., and Cohen, P.R. 1987. Design for acquisition: Principles of knowledge system design to facilitate knowledge acquisition. *International Journal of Man-Machine Studies, 26,* 143–159.

Hammond, K.J. 1989. *Case-based Planning: Viewing Planning as a Memory Task.* Boston: Academic Press. Based on doctoral dissertation, Computer Science Department, Yale University.

Hannan, J., and Politakis, P. 1985. ESSA: An approach to acquiring decision rules for diagnostic expert systems. *Proceedings of the Second Conference on Artificial Intelligence Applications* (pp. 520–525). Orlando, Florida: IEEE Computer Society Press.

Hayes-Roth, B. 1985. A blackboard architecture for control. *Artificial Intelligence, 26,* 251–321.

Hayes-Roth, B., Garvey, A., Johnson, M., and Hewett, M. 1987. *A layered environment for reasoning about action.* (Technical Report KSL 86-38). Stanford, CA: Computer Science Department, Stanford University.

Hayes-Roth, B., and Hewett, M. 1985. *Learning control heuristics in a blackboard environment.* (Technical Report HPP-85-2). Stanford, CA: Computer Science Department, Stanford University.

Hutchins, E.L., Hollan, J.D., and Norman, D.A. 1986. Direct manipulation interfaces. In D.A. Norman, and S.W. Draper (Eds.), *User centered system design.* Hillsdale, NJ: Lawrence Erlbaum Associates.

Johnson, N.E., and Tomlinson, C.M. 1988. Knowledge representation for knowledge elicitation. *Proceedings of the Third AAAI Knowledge Acquisition for Knowledge-based Systems Workshop,* Banff, Canada, November. Calgary, Alberta: SRDG Publications, Department of Computer Science, University of Calgary.

Kaelbling, L.P. 1987. An architecture for intelligent reactive systems. In M.P. Georgeff and A.L. Lansky (Eds.), *Reasoning About Actions and Plans, Proceedings of the 1986 Workshop at Timberline, Oregon* (pp. 411–424). Morgan Kaufmann.

Kassirer, J.P., and Gorry, G.A. 1978. Clinical problem solving: A behavioral analysis. *Annals of Internal Medicine, 89*, 245–255.

Kay, A. 1984. Computer software. *Scientific American, 251*, 52–59, September.

Keeney, R.L., and Raiffa, H. 1976. *Decisions with Multiple Objectives: Preferences and Value Tradeoffs.* John Wiley and Sons.

Keller, R.M. 1988. Defining operationality for explanation-based learning. *Artificial Intelligence, 35*, 227–241.

Klinker, G. 1988. KNACK: Sample-driven knowledge acquisition for reporting systems. In S. Marcus (Ed.), *Automating knowledge acquisition for expert systems.* Boston: Kluwer Academic Publishers.

Laird, J.D., Newell, A., and Rosenbloom, P.S. 1987. SOAR: An architecture for general intelligence. *Artificial Intelligence, 33*, 1–64.

Lenat, D.B., and Brown, J.S. 1984. Why AM and EURISKO appear to work. *Artificial Intelligence, 23*, 269–294.

Marcus, S. 1987. Taking backtracking with a grain of SALT. *International Journal of Man-Machine Studies, 24*, 383–398.

Marcus, S. 1988. SALT: A knowledge acquisition tool for propose-and-refine systems. In S. Marcus (Ed.), *Automating knowledge acquisition for expert systems.* Boston: Kluwer Academic Publishers.

McDermott, J. 1988. Preliminary steps toward a taxonomy of problem-solving methods. In S. Marcus (Ed.), *Automating knowledge acquisition for expert systems.* Boston: Kluwer Academic Publishers.

Minton, S., and Carbonell, J.G. 1987. Strategies for learning search control rules: An explanation-based approach. *Proceedings of the Tenth International Joint Conference on Artificial Intelligence*, Milan, Italy: Morgan Kaufmann.

Mitchell, T.M. 1982. Generalization as search. *Artificial Intelligence, 18*, 203–226.

Mitchell, T.M., Keller, R.M., and Kedar-Cabelli, S.T. 1986. Explanation-based generalization: A unifying view. *Machine Learning, 1*, 56–80.

Mitchell, T.M., Mahadevan, S., and Steinberg, L.I. LEAP: A learning apprentice for VLSI design. *Proceedings of the Ninth International Conference on Artificial Intelligence* (pp. 573–580). Los Angeles, CA: Morgan Kaufmann.

Mitchell, T.M., Utgoff, P.E., and Banerji, R.B. 1983. Learning by experimentation: Acquiring and refining problem-solving heuristics. In R.S. Michalski, J.G. Carbonell, and T.M. Mitchell (Eds.), *Machine Learning: An Artificial Intelligence Approach*, San Mateo, CA: Morgan Kaufmann.

Mostow, D.J. 1983. Machine transformation of advice into a heuristic search procedure. In R. Michalski, J. Carbonell, and T.M. Mitchell (Eds.), *Machine learning: An artificial intelligence approach.* San Mateo, CA: Morgan Kaufmann.

Morik, K. 1988. Sloppy modeling. In K. Morik (Ed.), *Knowledge representation and organization in machine learning.* Berlin: Springer-Verlag, in press.

Musen, M.A. 1989. *Automated Generation of Model-based Knowledge-Acquisition Tools*, London: Pitman. Based on doctoral dissertation, Computer Science Department, Stanford University.

Musen, M.A., Fagan, L.M., and Shortliffe, E.H. 1986. Graphical specification of procedural knowledge for an expert system. *Proceedings of the 1986 IEEE Computer Society Workshop in Visual Languages* (pp. 167–178). Dallas, Texas.

Musen, M.A., Fagan, L.M., Combs, D.M., and Shortliffe, E.H. 1987. Use of a domain model to drive an interactive knowledge editing tool. *International Journal of Man-Machine Studies, 26*, 105.

Neches, R., Swartout, W., and Moore, J. 1985. Enhanced maintenance and explanation of expert systems through explicit models of their development. *IEEE Transactions on Software Engineering, SE-11* (11), 1337–1351.

Newell, A. 1982. The knowledge level. *Artificial Intelligence, 18*, 87–127.

Nisbett, R., and Wilson, T. 1977. Telling more than we can know: Verbal reports on mental processes. *Psychological Review, 84*, 231–259.

Pauker, S.G., and Kassirer, J.P. 1981. Clinical decision analysis by personal computer. *Archives of Internal Medicine, 141*, 1831–1837.

Quinlan, J.R. 1983. Learning efficient classification procedures and their application to chess end games. In R. Michalski, J. Carbonell, and T. Mitchell (Eds.), *Machine learning: An artificial intelligence approach.* San Mateo, CA: Morgan Kaufmann.

Quinlan, J.R. 1986. Induction of decision trees. *Machine Learning*, *1* (1), 81–106.

Sacerdoti, E.D. 1974. Planning in a hierarchy of abstraction spaces. *Artificial Intelligence*, *5*, 115–135.

Shachter, R.D., and Heckerman, D.E. 1987. Thinking backward for knowledge acquisition. *AI Magazine 8*, 55–61.

Shaw, M.L.G., and Gaines, B. 1987. Techniques for knowledge acquisition and transfer. *International Journal of Man-Machine Studies*, *27*.

Shortliffe, E.H., Scott, A.C., Bischoff, M.B., van Melle, W., and Jacobs, C.D. 1981. ONCOCIN: An expert system for oncology protocol management. *Proceedings of the Seventh International Joint Conference on Artificial Intelligence* (pp. 876–881). Vancouver, British Columbia: Morgan Kaufmann.

Silver, B. 1986. *Metal-level Inference: Representing and Learning Control Information in Artificial Intelligence*. New York: North-Holland.

Sticklen, J., Chandrasekaran, B., and Josephson, J.R. 1985. Control issues in classificatory diagnosis. *Proceedings of the Ninth International Joint Conference on Artificial Intelligence* (pp. 300–306). Los Angeles, CA: Morgan Kaufmann.

Swartout, W. 1983. XPLAIN: A system for creating and explaining expert consulting systems. *Artificial Intelligence*, *11*, 115–144.

Tu, S.W., Kahn, M.G., Musen, M.A., Ferguson, J.C., Shortliffe, E.H., and Fagan, L.M. 1989. Episodic monitoring of time-oriented data for heuristic skeletal-plan refinement. *Communications of the ACM*, in press.

Utgoff, P. 1986. *Machine Learning of Inductive Bias*. Boston: Kluwer Academic Publishers. Based on doctoral dissertation, Department of Computer Science, Rutgers University.

Waterman, D.A. 1970. Generalization learning techniques for automating the learning of heuristics. *Artificial Intelligence*, *1*, 121–170.

Winograd, T., and Flores, F. 1987. *Understanding Computers and Cognition*. Reading, MA: Addison-Wesley.

Winston, P.H. 1985. Learning structural descriptions from examples. In P.H. Winston (Ed.), *The Psychology of Computer Vision*. New York: McGraw Hill.

Machine Learning, 4, 337–338 (1989)

The World Would Be a Better Place if Non-Programmers Could Program

JOHN McDERMOTT
Digital Equipment Corporation, 290 Donald Lynch Boulevard, DLB5-3/E2, Marlborough, MA 01752

Each task that anyone, man or machine, might want to perform imposes some set of computational requirements on the performer. This is obvious—how could it be otherwise? But if you ask anyone what the computational requirements are that a class of tasks imposes, you surely won't get a very good answer. As application programmers, we can expose the computational requirements of the task we just wrote a program to solve. But we typically do so by pointing to the program; this doesn't provide much insight, either to ourselves or to others, into the requirements that other, similar tasks impose. From the perspective of one who simply wants an understanding of the computational requirements of a class of tasks, the application program over-commits.

Over the years, AI researchers have had insights that can potentially improve this state of affairs. In particular, the idea that an inference engine (a control structure) can be defined that operates on domain knowledge to solve problems is a good starting point. An inference engine is precisely the set of mechanisms that satisfies the computational requirements of some class of tasks. Thus showing someone an inference engine, rather than a complete program, at least has the value that it is appropriately general. But there is still a problem. We don't have concepts that allow the computational requirements of tasks to be easily discussed. Another way of saying this is that no inference engine builder has yet been successful at defining, in terms understandable to those familiar with tasks, the characteristics a task has to have in order for it to be an appropriate task for his or her inference engine.

If we had such a set of concepts, we could develop a wide variety of useful and effective inference engines. Each engine would provide the computational mechanisms required to address a particular class of tasks—i.e., all tasks with a specific set of characteristics. Since each set of mechanisms presupposes the availability of certain types of information, the mechanisms effectively define the knowledge that has to be elicited from those familiar with the task. Moreover, since each set of mechanisms requires particular access paths to that information, the mechanisms effectively define how the knowledge can be appropriately represented. Thus such engines should substantially simplify the program development and maintenance process.

It should be easy to begin to invent the appropriate set of concepts. A task has characteristics that need attention whenever it is performed. For example, for a subset of diagnostic tasks, a critical task characteristic is the existence of competing possible explanations that must be discriminated among. Or for a subset of configuration tasks, a critical task characteristic is the existence of an ordered set of fixes that can be used to modify configurations that violate constraints. I'll call the concept that acknowledges the diagnostic task

91

characteristic the "competing explanations" concept. And I'll call the concept that acknowledges the configuration task characteristic the "obvious fix" concept. A set of mechanisms suggest themselves for each of these two characteristics.

For tasks involving competing explanations, two mechanisms suggest themselves: (1) a mechanism for identifying candidate explanations, and (2) a mechanism for evaluating candidate explanations relative to one another. For tasks involving obvious fixes, four mechanisms suggest themselves: (1) a mechanism that keeps track of component choices and why they were made (i.e., a dependency network), (2) a mechanism for identifying constraint violations, (3) a mechanism for retracting components that violate constraints, and (4) a mechanism for selecting components to substitute for retracted ones. The trick, of course, is getting the level of abstraction right so that no mechanism has to be further specialized in order to deal appropriately with a task instance, while at the same time each set of mechanisms comprising an engine covers as many task instances as possible.

For example, to say that the competing explanation characteristic requires a mechanism to evaluate candidate explanations is, of course, not an adequate specification since there are a number of such mechanisms more or less appropriate for different diagnostic tasks. But the important thing to note is that the number of mechanisms that produce interestingly different results is small. It matters whether the mechanism uses rule-in or rule-out as its primary strategy. It matters whether the mechanism treats evidence as having a likelihood or as having a threshold of relevance. It may matter whether evidence is arithmetically combined or not. And it matters whether the order in which questions are asked is determined by the expected cost of obtaining the information or by the expected value of the information. But for this mechanism, that's about all that matters. My bet is that getting to an appropriate level of abstraction for all mechanisms for all tasks requires specializations of approximately the same degree.

Machine Learning, 4, 339–345 (1989)

Task-Structures, Knowledge Acquisition and Learning

B. CHANDRASEKARAN   CHANDRA@CIS.OHIO-STATE.EDU
Laboratory for AI Research, Department of Computer and Information Science, The Ohio State University, Columbus, OH 43210

Abstract. One of the old saws about learning in AI is that *an agent can only learn what it can be told,* i.e., the agent has to have a vocabulary for the target structure which is to be acquired by learning. What this vocabulary is, for various tasks, is an issue that is common to whether one is building a knowledge system by learning or by other more direct forms of knowledge acquisition. I long have argued that both the forms of declarative knowledge required for problem solving as well as problem-solving strategies are functions of the *problem-solving task* and have identified a family of *generic tasks* that can be used as building blocks for the construction of knowledge systems. In this editorial, I discuss the implication of this line of research for knowledge acquisition and learning.

Key Words: Generic tasks, learning, knowledge acquisition, task-structure

1. Learning and Knowledge Acquisition

One of the more straightforward relations between knowledge acquisition and learning is that learning is one means of knowledge acquisition. But there is more to this relationship. One of the old saws about learning in AI is that *an agent can only learn what it can be told,* i.e., the agent has to have a vocabulary for the target structure which is to be acquired by learning. What this vocabulary is for various tasks is an issue that is common to whether one is building a knowledge system by learning or by other more direct forms of knowledge acquisition. For the last several years, my colleagues and I have been investigating *task-specific* architectures, in particular those that can support very general information-processing strategies that we have called *generic tasks* (GT's) [Chandrasekaran, 1986; 1987]. In this guest editorial, I would like to discuss the implication of this line of research for knowledge acquisition and learning.

Much of what I will say regarding the advantages for knowledge acquisition and learning of task-specific architectures is applicable not only to our particular work on generic tasks, but to other work in the task-specific spirit as well, e.g., the work of Marcus and McDermott [1989].

2. Generic Tasks

The GT view has been evolving, but the essence of the approach can be captured in the following ideas.

Problems, methods and subproblems. A problem (or a problem-solving goal) can have one or more *methods* associated with solving it (or achieving the goal). Each of the methods is characterized by forms of *knowledge* and *inference* that are necessary for carrying out the

93

method and by additional *subgoals* (or subproblems) that will need to be achieved (solved) in order to complete the application of the method for the problem. (A method can be a procedure where the sequencing of steps is all prespecified, but it can be more abstract; in Newell's problem space terminology [Newell, 1980], it can be a search in a problem space. In fact, such methods are the ones that are interesting from an AI point of view.)

For example, the problem of *classification* has a method called *hierarchical classification*, which consists of exploring the classification hypotheses organized as a hierarchy. This calls for knowledge in the form of *hierarchies* and inference methods which are variations of, and include as a default strategy, *top-down explorations* of the hierarchy. This method has subgoals in the form of *evaluating* the evidence for or against a hypothesis so that it can be established or rejected. This subgoal similarly can have many methods associated with it, each of which is characterized by its own knowledge and inference requirements.

GT's as problem/method/knowledge/inference packages. A combination of a problem/ method/knowledge/inference structure is something that we have called a *generic task* (GT). An underlying assumption of the GT view is that there are a number of generally useful GT's which serve as subgoals or subproblems for *many* complex knowledge-rich problem-solving tasks. For example, hierarchical classification is an ubiquitous method in diagnosis and selection problems. Similarly, *abstract plan instantiation and refinement* is an equally general method for parts of design or synthesis tasks. *Hierarchical abstraction of data* is another very useful method for concept matching or recognition.

A high level language for each GT. The GT approach has identified a number of such generally useful problem/method/knowledge/inference combinations and has made tools available that can support each such GT and combine them as building blocks in the solution of more complex problems. The support is provided in the form of knowledge and inference primitives appropriate for each method, in terms of which domain knowledge and inference can be directly encoded.

GT's and knowledge acquisition. The GT view enables the knowledge engineer to associate problems with appropriate methods and seek out the knowledge and inference patterns that are needed to support the method and also to access other GT's, i.e., problem/method/ knowledge/inference structures, that may be needed for any subproblems. Thus the GT view is a direct aid in knowledge acquisition, since it focuses the knowledge acquisition process on the operational knowledge and inference needs of the problem (or the task). How exactly the GT view helps in knowledge acquisition has been discussed at some length by Bylander and Chandrasekaran [Bylander and Chandrasekaran, 1987], but the idea is simple: the knowledge and inference primitives directly give the knowledge engineer a vocabulary in terms of which to seek both the declarative and control knowledge in the domain for the task.

Explanations of problem solving at the task level. The task-specific view in general and the GT view in particular give advantages by providing appropriate vocabularies in which explanations can be couched [Chandrasekaran, Tanner and Josephson, 1989]. Each of the methods can, in principle, explain its behavior by using the vocabulary of inference and control that is directly appropriate for it. When the right GT level tool is used to implement the method, the problem solver can "introspect" about its behavior at the level of abstraction that corresponds to that of the task. For example, the hierarchical classifier can explain its behavior using the language of establishing classificatory hypotheses and refining them,

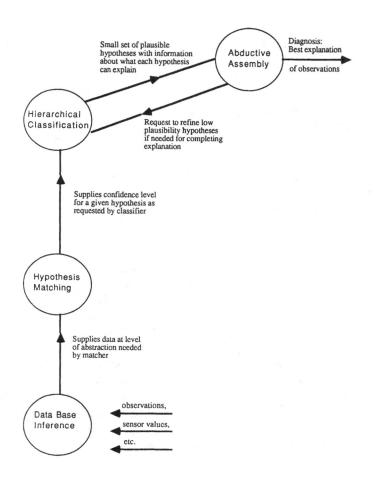

Figure 1. A generic task architecture for diagnosis with compiled knowledge.

and the plan instantiator and refiner can simply couch its behavior using a vocabulary of choosing between plans, invoking subplans, etc. If a diagnostic system is built using the generic tools for classification and hypothesis matching (see Figure 1), then the behavior of the diagnostic system can similarly be explained using the higher level explanatory vocabulary and a knowledge of the requirements of the task of diagnosis [Tanner, 1989].

3. Task Structures and Knowledge Acquisition

While I have talked in terms of generic tasks above, the points I am making are relevant for the more general notion of a *task-oriented methodology*. This methodology directs the process of analyzing and building knowledge-based systems for given problems by explicitly representing a *task-structure* for the problem[1]. This representation focuses the knowledge acquisition and system building stages by an explicit awareness of the requirements of the tasks in the task structure. A task structure is a representation of the task in terms of the methods that are applicable for it in the domain and the conditions under which each method is applicable. Each method is itself specified in terms of how it uses knowledge and inference to achieve its goals, and in terms of what subgoals it sets up and requires to be achieved before it can succeed. This kind of decomposition can be done recursively until methods which achieve subgoals but which do not set up additional subgoals of their own are reached. This task structure has an enormous amount of leverage in directing knowledge acquisition and system building, since the knowledge and inference requirements for the methods can be explicitly identified. In the GT methodology, the task analysis is aided by the fact that a number of generic subgoals and methods have been identified; this repertoire provides guidance in the task decomposition.

For example, in Figure 1, a task-structure for diagnosis is given in terms of a number of generic tasks. In many domains an applicable method for diagnosis is that of assembling a best explanation. This method sets up the subgoals of *generating highly plausible hypotheses* and *abductive assembly of hypotheses into a best explanation*. Generating highly plausible hypotheses can be done by the method of hierarchical classification, which in turn sets up a subgoal of *evaluating a confidence level* for each of the hypotheses in the hypothesis space. An applicable method for this evaluation is *hypothesis matching* in which data are abstracted through a hierarchy of intermediate abstractions of evidence and finally into evidence about the hypothesis. Notice that this methodology permits us to choose methods for subgoals that can be supported by domain knowledge. In domain A, knowledge may be available for hypothesis evaluation by evidence abstraction as indicated, while in domain B the goal may best be accomplished by the method of Bayesian probability calculations because knowledge is available in the form of prior and conditional probabilities. The task structure makes explicit how goals are to be accomplished by what types of knowledge and inference. Knowing the type of knowledge needed for each method in turn can give focus to the knowledge acquisition process.

4. Explanation-Based Learning

The task-oriented view in general and the GT approach in particular have significant potential to aid learning. In addition to the knowledge-type vocabulary that they provide for each task, their ability to generate explanations at the right level can give significant leverage for learning. Explanation-based learning, broadly construed, is a method of learning by constructing an explanation of why some solution was correct or incorrect, and using the explanation to define the concept that is being learned. I would like to outline how the explanatory capabilities of the GT approach are helpful for learning by briefly describing a work in this vein that is being conducted in my laboratory by Bylander and Weintraub [1988].

The research attempts to build a knowledge-based system that performs corrective learning. When its answer to a problem is incorrect, the system attempts to identify which part of the knowledge it used for which task in the task-structure may be at fault and also attempts to change it. In order to explain how this is intended to work, a brief description of the theory of task-specific explanation described in [Chandrasekaran et al., 1989] may be useful.

We identify three types of explanation relating to knowledge-based systems. These are: (1) trace of run-time, data-dependent problem-solving behavior, i.e., explaining how the data in the current situation was used to arrive at a decision; (2) relating specific decisions to the control strategy used by the system; and (3) justifying particular pieces of knowledge by relating them to more general domain knowledge.

Let us use the example of hierarchical classification in diagnosis to make the above ideas a little clearer. Let us say that diagnosis is performed by performing hierarchical classification on the malfunction hierarchy (Figure 2) and that the control strategy is that of top-down refinement. If a hypothesis is established, its successors are examined; if a hypothesis is rejected, its subtree is pruned. Type 1 explanation will involve showing how a hypothesis was established by pointing to which data contributed evidence for and against it—there may be different ways of establishing the concept, and we want to know how in this particular instance the concept was established. Type 2 explanation would involve, e.g., explaining that a concept was rejected because its parent had been ruled out—this rejection being a consequence of the control strategy used in hierarchical classification. Let us say that one of the pieces of knowledge used in hierarchical classification is that data d1, d2, and d3 indicate a certain malfunction M in the hierarchy. Type 3 explanation will involve justifying this knowledge itself, e.g., by appealing to a structural model of the system that is being diagnosed and showing how malfunction M actually causes observations d1, d2, and d3.

The diagnostic and learning system being built by Weintraub and Bylander works in the domain of pathologic gait analysis. This diagnostic system combines abductive assembly and hierarchical classification problem solvers as in Figure 1 with a qualitative model of gait. The human expert, during the learning mode of the system, evaluates the correctness of the answer given by the system. If the system's answer is incorrect, the expert also provides the correct answer.

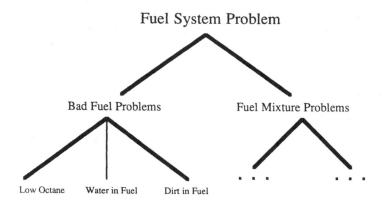

Fuel System Problem

Bad Fuel Problems

Fuel Mixture Problems

Low Octane   Water in Fuel   Dirt in Fuel

Figure 2. Example of a classification hierarchy.

Type 1 and Type 2 explanations can be constructed for the incorrect answer. Specifically, data used in support of bad judgments about individual hypotheses (Type 1) as well as how the control strategy led to errors (Type 2) can be constructed. Without getting into details, these explanations together can be used to identify possible knowledge elements that could have been responsible for the error, and which tasks in the task structure they are associated with. For example, the source of an incorrect decision may be traced to the fact that the evidence for a particular hypothesis is being incorrectly evaluated in the "Hypothesis Matching" subtask. Thus the explanation capability associated with the task-specific view helps solve some aspects of the *credit assignment problem* for learning.

The Type 3 explanation produced by the qualitative model can give additional pointers both for locating the possible places for the error as well as help in generating alternatives. Put another way, explanations of Types 1 and 2 help identify *what* is wrong, and Type 3 explanation will help identify *how* it is wrong. Thus the corrective learning is accomplished by a form of explanation-based learning, which in turn is made possible by the task-specific architectures that help specify how the task structure makes decisions.

5. Concluding Remarks

Understanding how learning can be used to build knowledge systems for problem solving involves uncovering both *general mechanisms* that play a role independent of the task or domain involved, e.g., *chunking* [Laird, Newell & Rosenbloom, 1987], as well as a specification of *what* needs to be learned for the problem at hand. Much of the interest in the field of knowledge systems has revolved around general, i.e., task-independent, architectures, which do not directly support distinctions in knowledge and inference for different types of tasks. There is a tendency to think of *all* knowledge as so much domain-specific details in this architecture, and hence to think that one cannot say interesting things, from an AI point of view, about learning this knowledge. On the other hand, we have discussed in this editorial task-specific but domain-independent information-processing strategies. A task-structure specifies how the problem at hand can be solved by using such generic tasks, and a theory of what knowledge needs to be acquired can be developed for these tasks. This level of abstraction directly helps in knowledge acquisition and, by providing explanations of problem solving that match the tasks, can help in learning.

Acknowledgments

The research reported is supported by Air Force Office of Scientific Report, grant 87-0090. I also thank Mike Weintraub and Tom Bylander for comments on an earlier draft.

Notes

1. A clarification of terms may be useful at this point. We have used the term "problem" to describe the task that a problem solving system is set, e.g., diagnosis, and the term "task" to refer to the more generic subproblems, e.g., classification, in the task-structure. This is for expository convenience and no absolute distinction is meant.

References

Bylander, T., and Chandrasekaran, B. 1987. Generic tasks for knowledge-based reasoning; The "right" level of abstraction for knowledge acquisition. *International Journal of Man-Machine Studies,* 26, 231–243.

Bylander, T. and Weintraub, M. 1988. A corrective learning procedure using different explanatory types. *AAAI Mini-Symposium on Explanation-Based Learning.* Stanford University, Palo Alto, CA.

Chandrasekaran, B. 1986. Generic tasks in knowledge-based reasoning; High-level building blocks for expert system design. *IEEE Expert, 1,* 23–30.

Chandrasekaran, B. 1987. Towards a functional architecture for intelligence based on generic information processing tasks. Invited talk, *Proceedings of the International Joint Conference on Artificial Intelligence.* IJCAI.

Chandrasekaran, B., Tanner, M. and Josephson, J. 1989. Explaining control strategies in problem solving. *IEEE Expert, 4,* 9–24.

Laird, J.E., Newell, A. and Rosenbloom, P.S. 1987. SOAR: An architecture for general intelligence. *Artificial intelligence, 33,* 1–64.

Marcus, S. and McDermott, J. 1989. SALT: A knowledge acquisition tool for propose-and-revise systems. *Artificial intelligence, 39,* 1–37.

Newell, A. 1980 Reasoning, problem solving and decision process: The problem space as a fundamental category. In L. Erlbaum (Eds.) *Attention and performance, VIII.*

Tanner, M. 1989. *Explaining knowledge systems: Justifying diagnostic conclusions.* Ph.D. thesis, Department of Computer and Information Science, The Ohio State University, Columbus, OH.

Machine Learning, 4, 347–375 (1989)

Automated Support for Building and Extending Expert Models

MARK A. MUSEN   MUSEN@SUMEX-AIM.STANFORD.EDU
Medical Computer Science Group, Knowledge Systems Laboratory, Stanford University, Stanford, California 94305-5479

Abstract. Building a knowledge-based system is like developing a scientific theory. Although a knowledge base does not constitute a theory of some natural phenomenon, it does represent a theory of how a class of professionals approaches an application task. As when scientists develop a natural theory, builders of expert systems first must formulate a model of the behavior that they wish to understand and then must corroborate and extend that model with the aid of specific examples. Thus there are two interrelated phases of knowledge-base construction: (1) model building and (2) model extension. Computer-based tools can assist developers with both phases of the knowledge-acquisition process. Workers in the area of knowledge acquisition have developed computer-based tools that emphasize either the building of new models or the extension of existing models. The PROTÉGÉ knowledge-acquisition system addresses these two activities individually and facilitates the construction of expert systems when the same general model can be applied to a variety of application tasks.

Key Words. knowledge acquisition, knowledge engineering, human–computer interaction, visual languages, domain modeling

1. Introduction

Knowledge acquisition is the process of eliciting the expertise of authorities in an application area and of formalizing that knowledge within a computer program. From the time of McCarthy's [1968] early proposal for the "Advice Taker" (a theoretical program that could act on the statements about the world that its users typed into it in predicate logic), workers in artificial intelligence (AI) have described tools that could facilitate the knowledge-acquisition process. Knowledge acquistion often is depicted as the cumbersome activity whereby expertise is transferred from the minds of application specialists to those of the computer scientists who build expert systems (knowledge engineers), and thence to the knowledge bases of expert systems. Most builders of knowledge-acquisition tools consequently perceive knowledge acquisition as a problem in *knowledge flow*.

The depiction of knowledge acquisition as the transfer of expertise has caused many researchers to view knowledge engineers as middlemen, whose naiveté in the application area impedes communication and clogs the pipeline during knowledge extraction. Davis' [1976] landmark knowledge-acquisition program, TEIRESIAS, was predicated on the proposition that, if domain experts could enter their knowledge directly into expert systems, the need for knowledge engineers during the refinement of new knowledge bases would be eliminated. Although Davis' suggestion was influential, TEIRESIAS never actually was used by the expert physicians for whom it was intended. During the more than one dozen years that have ensued since the development of TEIRESIAS, a score of computer-based

101

knowledge-acquisition tools have been constructed, most designed to eliminate the need for knowledge engineers [Boose 1989]. Despite this nearly universal goal, not one of these tools has supplanted the humans needed to assist application specialists in the construction and maintenance of production-quality expert systems [Kitto 1989]. Although current knowledge-acquisition tools may greatly facilitate the process, development of most expert systems still requires intermediaries and still is often bottlenecked.

The emphasis on knowledge transfer and the view of the knowledge engineer as an intermediary, however, have hindered the recognition that knowledge acquisition is a creative and inventive activity. When knowledge engineers interview application specialists to develop expert systems, they begin to form mental models of how the experts solve problems; the experts, of course, have mental models of their own that attempt to capture their professional problem-solving behavior. In the course of building the expert system, both the knowledge engineers and the experts continually revise their respective mental models. Although the knowledge engineers and the application specialists may have very different mental models at the outset of their collaboration, the models eventually converge. This convergence is possible (1) because the knowledge-acquisition process forces all parties to commit their mental models to a fixed, publicly examinable form—typically, the emerging knowledge base; and (2) because the frequent consideration of examples and test cases forces the system builders to assess, corroborate, and revise their models. The often-cited difficulties of knowledge acquisition can be ascribed, in general, to creating and agreeing on a shared model of problem solving [Winograd and Flores 1986; Regoczei and Plantinga 1987].

The creation of a knowledge base is much like the creation of a scientific theory. Unlike traditional scientists, however, builders of expert systems are not concerned with the elaboration of theories of natural phenomena; these knowledge engineers instead seek to develop theories of expert behavior. In constructing a knowledge base, system builders first define a general model (or theory) of the application task to be performed. In the case of the MYCIN system [Buchanan and Shortliffe 1984], for example, that general task model was one of diagnosing and treating infectious diseases. Given the initial model, MYCIN's developers validated and revised that model as necessary, attempting to fit the model to specific clinical problems. Once the essential model was worked out, it was then extended to include knowledge of particular kinds of bacteremia and, later, of meningitis. For example, after the basic system had been designed, the developers of MYCIN augmented the program's knowledge base to permit diagnosis and treatment of bacterial, fungal, viral, and tuberculous meningitis by making four separate extensions to the original MYCIN model.

Thus knowledge acquisition can be viewed as comprising two interrelated phases: (1) building a general task model—that is, creating an *intention* of the proposed system's behavior, followed by (2) filling in the specific content knowledge in the domain that is consistent with the general model—that is, creating *extensions* [Addis 1987]. In this paper, I shall discuss the special nature of these two stages of knowledge acquisition, with an emphasis on the kinds of computer-based tools that can facilitate the two phases. Knowledge-acquisition systems such as ROGET [Bennett 1985] are *model-building* tools that are particularly well suited to help knowledge engineers and application specialists to develop theories of expert problem solving. Other systems, such as OPAL [Musen, et al. 1987], are *model-extending* tools that are best used by domain experts working along to define specific applications. Recent work on the PROTÉGÉ knowledge-acquisition system [Musen 1989a, b] demonstrates how a model-building tool can help knowledge engineers to fashion a general task model, such that that model then can be used by a second model-extending tool to permit experts to define specific applications. In particular, PROTÉGÉ allows system builders to create general models of application tasks that can be solved with the method of skeletal-plan refinement [Friedland and Iwasaki 1985]; PROTÉGÉ then generates automatically knowledge-acquisition tools like OPAL that domain experts can use to enter the content knowledge for individual applications.

2. The Problem of Creating Models

Computer-based knowledge-acquisition tools, unlike traditional machine-learning programs, assume that knowledge will be formalized as the consequence of an interaction with a human expert. This interaction, which undeniably constitutes the greatest strength of the knowledge-engineering approach, also is the source of substantial liability. Application specialists cannot simply transfer their expertise to a computer, and knowledge-acquisition programs often cannot accept an expert's entries at face value. Understanding why a direct transfer of expertise is impossible both points to a major distinction between current research in knowledge acquisition and work in machine learning, and motivates important design decisions made in the construction of PROTÉGÉ.

Like the construction of other large pieces of software, the engineering of knowledge-based systems requires significant creativity on the part of system builders. Creativity is essential because the application specialists whose professional acumen is to be encoded as a knowledge base often cannot verbalize how they actually go about solving problems. Experts may not be merely inarticulate in explaining their behavior; they frequently are tongue-tied for reasons stemming from the very nature of human intelligence.

2.1. The Paradox of Expertise

Human cognitive skills appear to be acquired in at least three generally distinct stages of learning [Fitts 1964; LaBerge and Samuels 1974; Johnson 1983]. Although different authors have used different terms to describe the three phases, there is concordance regarding the qualitative changes that occur in the way that people seem to retrieve information during problem solving. Initially, there is the *cognitive* stage, during which an individual identifies the actions that are appropriate in particular circumstances, either as a result of direct instruction or from observation of other people. In this stage, the learner often verbally rehearses information needed for execution of the skill. Next comes the *associative* phase of learning, in which the relationships noted during the cognitive stage are practiced and verbal mediation begins to disappear. With repetition and feedback, the person begins to apply the actions accurately in a fluent and efficient manner. Then, in the final *autonomous* stage, the learner *compiles* the relationships from repeated practice to the point where he can perform them without conscious awareness. Suddenly, the person performs the actions appropriately, proficiently, and effortlessly—without thinking. The knowledge has become *tacit* [Fodor 1968].

There is substantial evidence that, as humans become experienced in an application area and repeatedly apply their know-how to specific tasks, their knowledge becomes compiled and thus inaccessible to their consciousness. Experts lose awareness of what they know. The knowledge that experts acquired as novices may be retrievable in a *declarative* form, yet the skills that these professionals actually practice are *procedural* in nature [Anderson 1987]. Although there is no consensus on how such procedural knowledge is stored within the nervous system [Rumelhart and Norman 1983], the inability of experts to verbalize these compiled associations is well accepted [Nisbett and Wilson 1977; Lyons 1986]. The consequence is that the special knowledge that we would most like to incorporate into our expert systems often is that knowledge about which experts are least able to talk. Johnson [1983] has identified this phenomenon as *the paradox of expertise*.

The paradox is confirmed by experimental data, as well as by much acecdotal experience. Johnson [1983], for example, reports that he once enrolled in classes at the University of Minnesota Medical School as part of his investigation of the process of medical diagnosis. At the same time, Johnson had the opportunity to study a medical colleague (one of his teachers) caring for patients on the hospital wards. Johnson compared the physician's observed clinical behavior with the diagnostic methods his colleague was teaching in the classroom. To Johnson's surprise, the medical-school professor's behavior in practice seemed to contradict what the teacher professed. When confronted with these observations, Johnson's subject responded:

> Oh, I know that, but you see I don't know how I actually do diagnosis, and yet I need to teach things to students. I create what I think of as plausible means of doing tasks and hope students will be able to convert them into effective ones. [Johnson 1983, p. 81]

The clinician in this example recognized explicitly that he could not verbalize his compiled expertise in medical diagnosis. The problem for knowledge engineers and for builders of knowledge-acquisition tools, however, is that people rarely know the limits of their tacit knowledge. When asked to report on their compiled expertise, subjects often volunteer plausible answers that may well be incorrect. In experimental situations, subjects have been shown to be frequently (1) unaware of the existence of a stimulus or cue influencing a response, (2) unaware that a response has been affected by a stimulus, and (3) unaware that a cognitive response has even occurred. Instead, subjects give verbal reports of their cognition based on prior causal theories from their nontacit memory [Nisbett and Wilson 1977]. Furthermore, because Western culture mistakenly teaches us that accurate introspection somehow should be possible [Lyons 1986], people freely explain and rationalize their compiled behaviors without recognizing that these explanations frequently are incorrect.

2.2. Authentic and Reconstructed Strategies

When asked questions about tacit processes, experts volunteer plausible answers that may not reflect their true behavior. These believable, although sometimes inaccurate, responses are known as *reconstructed* reasoning methods [Johnson 1983]. Reconstructed methods typically are acknowledged and endorsed by entire problem-solving communities. They form the basis of most major textbooks. The disadvantage of these methods, however, is that they do not always work. Slovic and Lichtenstein [1971], for example, asked stock brokers to weight the importance of various factors that influenced these brokers' investment decisions. A regression analysis of *actual* decisions made by the stock brokers revealed computed weights for these factors that were poorly correlated with the brokers' subjective ratings. More important, there was a *negative* correlation between the accuracy of introspection and the stock brokers' years of experience. More recently, Michalski and Chilausky [1980] found that decision rules elicited from plant pathologists for the diagnosis of soybean diseases performed less accurately than did a rule set that was automatically induced by application of the AQ11 algorithm to a library of test cases. (The experts' actual diagnoses were used as the gold standard against which the two sets of rules were judged.)

Many workers in knowledge acquisition have consequently argued for the elicitation of *authentic* (as opposed to reconstructed) methods of reasoning in hopes of improving expert-system performance [Johnson 1983; Cleaves 1987; Meyer, et al. 1989]. The goal is determination of the behaviors actually used by experts in performing relevant tasks. Acquisition of authentic knowledge, not surprisingly, requires more than just posing direct questions and asking application experts to introspect. Despite intense research to develop non-biasing interviewing techniques [for example, Ericsson and Simon 1984], psychometric methods [for example, Cooke and McDonald 1987], and ethnographic approaches [for example, Belkin et al., 1987], the elicitation of authentic problem-solving strategies remains cumbersome and often is impractical. The translation of authentic reasoning methods (when such methods can be elicited) into current knowledge-system architectures in a manner that avoids artifacts due to the knowledge-representation language itself also is an unsolved problem.

Knowledge engineers, therefore, must apprehend both the authentic and the reconstructed knowledge derived from application specialists and must assess that knowledge objectively. The engineers serve the important function of detecting gaps in the knowledge and of helping the application specialists to fill those gaps by defining plausible sequences of actions that can achieve the necessary goals. Knowledge engineers thus create theories of how the experts tacitly solve problems. The knowledge bases that embody those theories may not achieve the same level of performance as do the procedures actually used by domain experts, but the knowledge bases nevertheless can be observed, extended, and easily disseminated to other people in need of advice. It is incorrect to view a knowledge base as an embodiment of some human's problem-solving expertise. Knowledge bases instead represent only *models* of expert behavior—models that attempt to approximate, but that do not reproduce, the actual problem-solving steps used by humans [Clancey 1986].

When attempting to automate knowledge acquisition, we must identify the roles that knowledge engineers—and that computer-based tools—can play in either the creation or the extension of expert models. The PROTÉGÉ system has been developed under the premise that, at present, it is neither possible nor desirable to build tools to automate the entire knowledge-acquisition process. We can find data in support of that proposition by examining how knowledge engineers and experts have tried to use previous knowledge-acquisition tools to develop practical knowledge bases. Some automated tools help system developers to craft a model of the application task to be performed. Other tools assume that a model of the task area already exists. We now consider these two classes of knowledge-acquisition programs in detail.

3. Tools for Creating Task Models

When building an expert system, developers must first perform a requirements analysis and must identify the *task* that the expert system will perform. Then, knowledge engineers and application specialists traditionally must work together to construct a model of the proposed system's behavior. This model generally corresponds to the developers' theory of how the expert actually solves problems. Much of the necessary modeling activity entails what Newell [1982] refers to as *knowledge-level analysis*—determining (1) the goals for an intelligent system, (2) the actions of which the system is capable, and (3) the knowledge that the system can use to select actions that can achieve the goals. The process of knowledge-level analysis makes no assumptions about the set of symbols with which the expert system ultimately will be encoded (that is, about the rules, frames, or other data structures within the knowledge-representation language). The concern at this stage is only the *behaviors* of which the system will be capable.

There is increasing agreement in the literature that system builders should model the behavior of a proposed system at the knowledge level before they begin to implement the system. One modeling approach centers on defining abstract, domain-independent strategies known as *problem-solving methods* that can form the basis of languages that system builders can use to describe specific application tasks [Clancey 1985; McDermott 1988]. For example, Clancey's [1985] model of the method of *heuristic classification* includes abstract notions such as (1) *conclusions* that the problem solver may select from a pre-enumerated set, (2) *solution-refinement hierarchies* that allow the problem solver to narrow down the set of conclusions that it makes, (3) *data-abstraction hierarchies* that allow the problem solver to generalize from specific input data, and (4) *heuristics* that link abstractions of the user's input data to potential solutions.

Clancey derived the heuristic-classification model from a retrospective analysis of the behavior of a number of expert systems. Knowledge engineers, however, can apply such models of problem solving *prospectively* when they create new knowledge bases, structuring and clarifying the models that they create. Given an application task, such as MYCIN's task of identifying potential causes of infectious disease, developers can use the domain-independent concepts in the heuristic-classification model to define the intended behavior of an evolving system without reference to individual data structures that might be required to implement that behavior within the computer. By relating task-specific knowledge (such as attributes of possible infectious deseases) to well-understood problem-solving methods (such as the method of heuristic classification), developers clarify the roles that the knowledge plays in the system's production of recommendations, facilitating both the encoding and the maintenance of that system [McDermott 1988].

Researchers in AI have identified a number of domain-independent problem-solving methods that can assist system builders in the creation of knowledge-level models [Clancey 1985; Chandrasekaran 1986; McDermott 1988]. Considerable work concentrates on the elucidation of still other models of problem solving, particularly methods that might be applied to tasks that cannot be performed using classification. Although there is increasing consensus on the importance of the modeling approach, the knowledge-acquisition literature is fragmented by the use of inconsistent terminology. For example, whereas many researchers use the term *problem-solving method* for these abstract strategies [Clancey 1985; McDermott

1988; Boose 1989; Musen 1989c], workers at Ohio State University advocate the term *generic task* [Chandrasekaran 1986]. Yet most authors use the word *task* (without the "generic" modifier) to refer to an application problem to be solved. Unfortunately, the distinction between a *task* and a *generic task* often confuses both readers and authors. The developers of the KADS system for knowledge acquisition [Breuker and Wielinga 1987] use the expression *interpretation model* to refer to the formalization of a problem-solving method. In this paper, I consistently use the expression *problem-solving method*—or simply *method*— when referring to an abstract solution mechanism. The term *task* denotes the statement of an application problem, without regard to how that problem might be solved.

A source of additional confusion may arise in this paper, however, because there often are two kinds of models under discussion. First, there are models of *methods*, which represent sets of both terms and relationships for describing abstract, domain-independent solution strategies. Second, there are models of *tasks*, which represent terms and relationships for defining application problems to be solved. Frequently, system builders use the terms and relationships of a model of a problem-solving method (for example, heuristic classification) to define the specific terms and relationships that are needed to model an application task (for example, organism identification in MYCIN). If the task can be solved using the method, then the model of the method can provide a structure for the model of the task. Indeed, task models often can be viewed as direct extensions (or instantiations) of models of problem-solving methods [Musen 1989c].

Recently, several workers have developed computer-based knowledge-acquisition tools that expand this notion of relating task-specific knowledge to a predefined model of a problem-solving method [for example, Bennett 1985; Eshelman 1988; Marcus 1988]. Each of these tools presupposes a model of a different problem-solving method. Knowledge engineers use the terms and relationships in these models of problem solving to create new models for the solution of application *tasks* (Figure 1). In this paper, I refer to these method-oriented programs as *model-building* tools, because these tools help their users to devise and refine task models. To create the task models, users *extend* a pre-existing model of some problem-solving method. Each extension defines how the domain-independent method can be used to solve a particular application task.

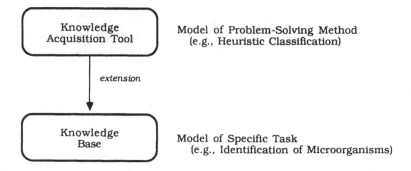

Figure 1. Creating a task model. Knowledge-acquisition tools such as ROGET contain models of domain-independent problem-solving methods. Users of such tools extend the problem-solving models to define specific application tasks.

ROGET [Bennett 1985], for example, was a knowledge-acquisition tool that contained a model of diagnosis that was a specialized form of heuristic classification. The program asked its user to identify the *problems* to be diagnosed, the *causes* of those problems, and the *data* that could be used to suggest, to confirm, or to rule out those causes and problems. A user's dialog with ROGET created a knowledge-level specification of the application task, which was then translated into EMYCIN symbols that could form the basis of a working consultation program. The knowledge engineer, however, modeled the application task (for example, the organism-identification task in MYCIN) in terms of the abstract notions of "problems," "causes," and "data." The developer never had to think in terms of the production rules or other data structures that EMYCIN ultimately would require to generate the proper diagnostic behavior.

A number of analogous method-based tools have been described subsequently, including MORE [Kahn, Nowlan, and McDermott 1985], MOLE [Eshelman 1988], and SALT [Marcus 1988]. PROTÉGÉ (which I shall describe in Section 5) is also of this class. Each of these tools provides a language that allows its users to create models of how application tasks can be solved. In each case, that language is one of a particular problem-solving method. Like ROGET, both MORE and MOLE assume that a user's task can be solved using a specialized form of heuristic classification. PROTÉGÉ and SALT, on the other hand, adopt problem-solving methods in which the solution is constructed. The method assumed by PROTÉGÉ is a specialized form of skeletal-plan refinement [Friedland and Iwasaki 1985]. The method built into SALT is a constraint-satisfaction strategy known as *propose and revise*.

Tools such as MORE, MOLE, and SALT allow their users to do much more than to create models of application tasks. Users of these tools also *extend* the task models that they develop with the many domain-specific facts that are necessary to generate complete knowledge bases. Unlike PROTÉGÉ, these other tools do not sharply distinguish between the activities of building models and those of extending them. However, because the process of task-model extension is necessarily preceded by that of task-model creation, it is appropriate to view such method-based tools as knowledge-acquisition aids that assist users in building task models.

In principle, all these model-building tools can be used by domain experts working alone. Indeed, mechanical engineers used SALT to develop an expert system that configures elevators for new buildings [Marcus 1988]. Such method-based tools, however, are used most effectively by knowledge engineers [Musen 1989c]. The terms and relationships of the problem-solving models assumed by the tools (for example, terms in ROGET such as "problems" and "causes") have precise semantics—distinct from these terms' vernacular meanings—that may not be clear to untrained users. A naive user who recognizes such terms as familiar lexical entities, but who may not appreciate the subtleties of the problem-solving model that the terms denote, will be incapable of translating his mental model of a domain task into an effective knowledge base. More important, the tacit nature of human expertise often makes it difficult for application specialists independently to develop robust models of their own behavior. For example, Kitto [1989] reports that when domain experts attempted to use the KNACK knowledge-acquisition tool [Klinker 1988] without the aid of knowledge engineers, the experts' inability to create models of the tasks to be performed constituted a major stumbling block. The entry of instantiating knowledge to extend task models that already had been developed with help from knowledge engineers, however, was much more straightforward for these experts.

4. Tools for Extending Task Models

Regardless of whether a computer-based tool is used to help developers to fashion the task model, after a knowledge engineer and domain expert have created a model of the intended behavior of the expert system, that model must be validated. An important form of validation is to ascertain how well the model applies to closely related application tasks. For example, given a task model that correctly identifies the presence of infections involving one class of micro-organism, system builders will want to confirm that the model can be extended to identify additional classes of potential pathogens. In this phase of knowledge acquisition, the developers test their model by establishing how that model applies to new situations. The system builders' original knowledge-level model is an *intention* of how problem solving occurs; each specific situation for which the model can be shown to apply is an *extension* of that model.[1]

Although creating a knowledge base may be difficult, extending an existing model is less cognitively taxing. Whereas experts may not be able to introspect and to articulate the *process knowledge* that allows them to solve problems [Johnson 1983; Winograd and Flores 1986], these experts certainly are adept at volunteering the *content knowledge* that may be either consistent or inconsistent with a given model. For example, a physician may not be able to provide a coherent description of how he actually diagnoses infectious diseases, but he may be able to describe readily the differences between bacterial and fungal meningitis. Thus, although knowledge engineers typically are needed to help to craft an initial task model, application experts may require little assistance either in extending an existing model or in identifying specific situations in which a given model fails. The frequently raised concern that the experts may not articulate authentic knowledge becomes moot when the specification of only content knowledge is at issue.

The automated knowledge-acquisition tools that are most suited for direct use by domain experts consequently are those that ask their users to extend existing models, rather than to create new ones [Musen 1989c]. Such tools both assume a predefined problem-solving method and incorporate a model of a *class* of application tasks; users extend the general task model to define specific applications (Figure 2). Unlike the detailed task models that knowledge engineers create and extend using tools such as MOLE and SALT, the task models that developers build into this latter set of model-extending knowledge-acquisition tools remain relatively abstract; the models are *intentions*. Rather than describing a particular task to be performed, these models define the characteristics of classes of application tasks that users might want to specify.

An example of such a tool is OPAL [Musen, et al. 1987], which was built by our laboratory to streamline knowledge acquisition for a medical expert system known as ONCOCIN [Tu, et al. 1989]. OPAL contains a model of the general task of administering cancer therapy and asks physicians to extend that model to specific cancer-therapy plans. OPAL's task model presupposes that patients will be treated with groups of drugs called *chemotherapies*. OPAL

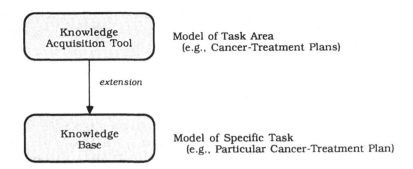

Figure 2. Extending a task model. Knowledge acquisition tools such as OPAL contain models of application-task areas. Users of tools such as OPAL extend the general task models to define specific applications (for example, particular cancer-treatment plans).

does not require its user to stipulate how chemotherapies are administered; such a model was developed by the knowledge engineers who built OPAL. Rather, the program asks its physician-user only to identify the sequence of chemotherapies in a particular treatment plan, to enter the doses of the relevant drugs, and to indicate how the administration of chemotherapy must be modified in response to changes in a patient's condition. Although the individual treatment plans are complex, the pre-existing task model reduces the process of defining new cancer treatments to simply filling in the blanks of graphical forms from menus (Figure 3), or to piecing together sequences of icons using a graphical flowchart language [Figure 4; Musen, et al. 1988]. OPAL thus solicits from the user an extension to its predefined task model that specifies a new treatment plan; the program then automatically generates from that extension a knowledge base that can be interpreted by the ONCOCIN system to carry out that plan.

The task model in OPAL makes assumptions regarding everything from the nature of chemotherapy to the kinds of conditions that can mandate modifications to a physician's treatment plan. Such assumptions define a *closed world*. There is no way to add new concepts to the model. OPAL allows physicians to create novel instantiations of existing concepts (for example, a user can readily define a previously unknown drug or chemotherapy), but the general classes of concepts in the model are predetermined. The task model tends to be sufficient, however, because of the highly stylized nature of cancer therapy. Because the terms in the model have precise, intuitive meanings that match the physicians' common usage of these terms, it is relatively simple for application specialists to fill in the blanks and to connect the flowchart icons in proper sequence to define new therapies. In 1986 alone, physicians used OPAL to enter 36 cancer-treatment plans. Each plan could be entered in a few hours or days. Previously, knowledge engineers and cancer specialists had typically required several weeks of work to encode each such plan using traditional, manual techniques.

System builders construct tools such as OPAL with the assumption that they will create multiple extensions to a given task model (for example, that they will create multiple chemotherapy knowledge bases). It would not be practical to incur the expense of programming such a tool if the system were not to be used repeatedly. There are a number of application areas where knowledge engineers have built tools to facilitate the construction of multiple,

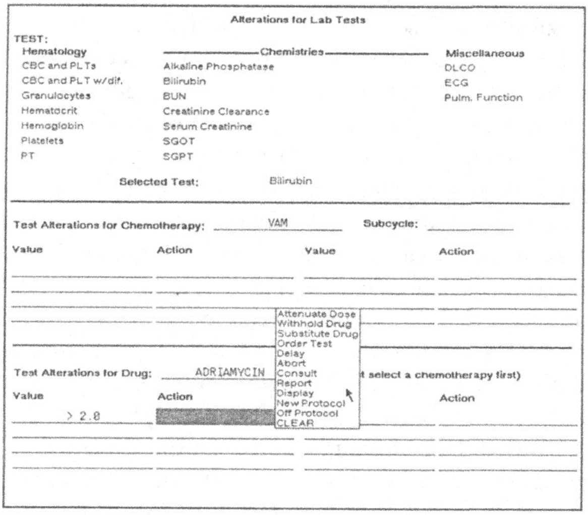

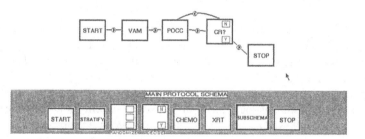

Figure 3. OPAL form for actions related to laboratory-test results. In this form, the physician is specifying how therapy should be modified if the level of bilirubin in a patient's blood is elevated to more than 2.0 mg/dl.

Figure 4. OPAL flowchart language. OPAL allows physicians to create visual programs corresponding to the procedural specification of chemotherapies (CHEMO) and X-ray therapies (XRT) in a given cancer-treatment plan. Below the region where the flowchart is entered is a palette of reference icons, used to add new nodes to the graph. The specification that has been entered in this figure calls for a single course of VAM chemotherapy to be given, followed by administration of POCC chemotherapy until the parameter CR (complete response) becomes *true*.

related knowledge bases. For example, Freiling and Alexander [1984] developed INKA to aid knowledge acquisition for an expert system that troubleshoots electronic instruments; each knowledge base created with INKA specifies fault-detection strategies for diagnosing a particular device. Similarly, Gale [1987] built a program called Student to aid knowledge acquisition for an expert system that advises researchers on the use of data-analysis programs; each knowledge base produced with Student specifies the use of a different statistical routine. In diverse domains such as medical therapy, event scheduling, and process control, system builders would benefit from tools such as OPAL that allow application experts to work alone, extending pre-existing task models to specify the knowledge that defines new task instances.

Although model-extending tools such as OPAL can be powerful in allowing domain specialists to author large knowledge bases without the concurrent need for knowledge engineers, each such tool is necessarily tied to a specific task model. For example, if someone is not interested in constructing a knowledge base for cancer chemotherapy, OPAL is useless to him. Tools such as OPAL can play a significant role in the life cycle of expert systems when developers require multiple knowledge bases for sets of related domain tasks. The challenge for tool builders is to recognize appropriate application areas and to generate such domain-specific programs rapidly and efficiently.

Building the models that form the basis of systems such as OPAL and Student is itself a problem in knowledge acquisition. Constructing such task-specific tools thus constitutes another kind of bottleneck. OPAL, for example, required 3.5 person-years to develop before any knowledge bases could be encoded. Building OPAL was cumbersome because, whenever developers altered their model of cancer therapy, OPAL had to be reprogrammed. More important, because that task model was not represented explicitly within OPAL, refining the model required kowledge engineers to modify LISP expressions throughout the system's program code; there was no knowledge-level representation of the model. These obstacles to maintaining OPAL, and the desire to transfer the methodology to application areas other than cancer therapy, prompted the development of PROTÉGÉ.

5. Generation of Tools that Extend Task Models

A tool for *building* task models (such as ROGET), which presupposes a particular problem-solving method, is best used by knowledge engineers to create knowlede-level models of the tasks that expert systems will perform. On the other hand, a tool for *extending* task models (such as OPAL), which presupposes a particular set of application tasks, can be used by application experts independently to define specific task instances. The two classes of tools are each suited for distinct phases of the expert-system life cycle. Because model building is invariably followed by model extension—and because the process of model extension often uncovers deficiencies in the original model that need to be repaired—an important goal is to make the use of these two types of tools as integrated as possible. An example of the necessary integration has been achieved with the research system called PROTÉGÉ [Musen 1989a, b].

5.1. The PROTÉGÉ System

PROTÉGÉ is a knowledge-acquisition tool that, like ROGET, assumes a particular problem-solving method—namely, a variant of skeletal-plan refinement [Friedland and Iwasaki 1985]. In performing skeletal planning, a problem solver decomposes a problem's abstract (skeletal) solution into one or more constituent plans that are each worked out in more detail than is the abstract plan. These constituent plans, however, may themselves be skeletal in nature and may require further distillation into subcomponents that are more fleshed out. The refinement process continues until a concrete solution to the problem is achieved.

The expert systems that PROTÉGÉ ultimately constructs produce as their output fully instantiated plans for their users to follow. In the cancer-chemotherapy domain, for example, such plans provide the details of the treatment that physicians should prescribe for an individual patient at specific stages of therapy. The method of skeletal-plan refinement has been applied to practical tasks not only in the ONCOCIN system [Tu, et al. 1989], but also in Friedland's [1979] MOLGEN program and in various versions of the Digitalis Therapy Advisor [Silverman 1975; Swartout 1981]. The method is well suited for applications that require construction of solutions for which the problem solver's reasoning does not need to concentrate on the details of selecting and ordering individual plan operators. In tasks that can be solved by skeletal-plan refinement, the availability of substantial domain knowledge makes it possible for the nuances of operator selection and of constraint satisfaction to be precompiled into the skeletal plans themselves. The problem-solving method consequently avoids search in favor of the instantiation of predefined partial plans [Friedland and Iwasaki 1985].

PROTÉGÉ allows a system builder to create an explicit model of a set of application tasks that can be solved by skeletal-plan refinement. PROTÉGÉ then *generates automatically* a knowledge-acquisition tool like OPAL that is custom-tailored for the set of application tasks that was modeled (Figure 5). PROTÉGÉ recently has been used to construct *p-OPAL*, a knowledge-acquisition tool for the cancer-therapy domain that reproduces the functionality of OPAL. A second program created using PROTÉGÉ, called *HTN*, allows physicians to enter treatment plans for the management of patients with hypertension [Musen 1989a]. Unlike OPAL, which required many months to program by hand, both p-OPAL and HTN were generated with PROTÉGÉ after only a few days of work.

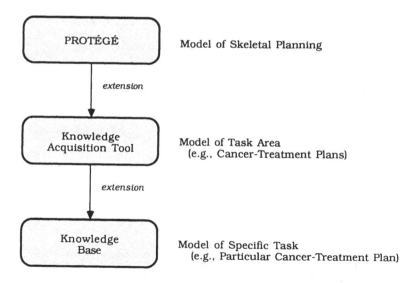

Figure 5. Creating and extending task models with PROTÉGÉ. Knowledge engineers extend the model of skeletal-plan refinement in PROTÉGÉ to create general task models; the application-specific tools that PROTÉGÉ generates then allow domain experts to extend those task models to define individual applications.

With PROTÉGÉ, a knowledge engineer defines a task model by filling out a series of graphical forms in a manner similar to the way in which oncologists fill out the forms in OPAL. As in OPAL, the PROTÉGÉ forms cluster together related information for presentation to the user and allow data to be examined and edited using direct-manipulation techniques. Although both PROTÉGÉ and OPAL acquire knowledge using hypermedia interfaces [Conklin 1987] and share common styles of human–computer interaction, the nature of the knowledge that users enter into the two systems is quite different. Whereas OPAL acquires knowledge of specific application tasks, PROTÉGÉ acquires knowledge of general task areas. Users enter into OPAL knowledge that is expressed in terms of that program's predefined model of cancer-therapy administration. The knowledge that users enter into PROTÉGÉ, on the other hand, is couched in terms of a predefined model of skeletal-plan refinement.

When PROTÉGÉ is first activated, the system's main menu appears on the workstation screen (Figure 6). This form allows access to other PROTÉGÉ forms that are available at the next organizational level. Via the main menu, the user can cause forms to be displayed that allow him to enter and edit the terms and relationships in a task model.

Figure 6. PROTÉGÉ main-menu form. This form asks the user for the name of the knowledge-editing system for which specifications are to be entered or edited using PROTÉGÉ. Once the name has been entered via the pop-up menu, the user can access forms for various topics by selecting the blanks in the menu. The top three items (PLANNING ENTITIES, TASK-LEVEL ACTIONS, and INPUT DATA) correspond to the three principal components of PROTÉGÉ's model of skeletal planning.

Task models created using PROTÉGÉ have the same three general components as does the cancer-therapy task model that was hand-coded into OPAL: (1) the *planning entities* in the domain from which the target expert system will refine its skeletal plans (for example, concepts such as the administration *chemotherapies* and *drugs* in oncology), (2) *actions* that can modify the application of one of the planning entities (for example, concepts such as *attenuating* the dose of a drug or *delaying* treatment), and (3) *input data* that will be entered by the user of the target expert system, the values of which may determine whether any of the *actions* should be applied (for example, concepts such as *laboratory-test results*).

The challenge for PROTÉGÉ users is to create a model of the task area under consideration that can be represented using the terms and relationships of the predefined skeletal-planning model. The knowledge engineer and domain specialist thus must examine the application area and discern the kinds of abstract plans that experts may construct. The developers then map the components of those plans into a hierarchy of PROTÉGÉ *planning entities* and establish the attributes of those plan components that are relevant during problem solving. The users also must determine how experts may modify the standard plans in the task area on the basis of external conditions, modeling such potential plan alterations as a set of PROTÉGÉ task *actions*. Finally, the knowledge engineer and application specialist must consider those external features that may bear on the system's recommendations. These features are modeled as *input data* in PROTÉGÉ's terminology. The PROTÉGÉ interface assists the developers by providing an explicit structure and a convenient notation for recording the components of the task model. Nevertheless, knowledge engineers and application specialists still must collaborate using traditional techniques to elucidate that model in the first place.

The mechanics of entering a task model in PROTÉGÉ are straightforward. For example, selecting PLANNING ENTITIES from the main menu in Figure 6 causes PROTÉGÉ to display the corresponding form for defining the components of skeletal plans in the relevant application domain. Figure 7 shows this planning-entities form filled out for the hypertension-therapy task, as was done to produce the HTN knowledge-editing tool. In the figure, the knowledge engineer has specified that the most general component of a plan is called a *protocol*, and that a problem solver may refine hypertension protocols into more detailed plans that entail the prescription of *tablets*, the ordering of *tests*, and the passage of *wait* periods. The specifications for these components say nothing about the particular kinds of tablets that might be prescribed or the precise tests that might be ordered during the administration of a particular treatment protocol for high blood pressure; the specifications form only an *intention* of the application tasks that are possible in the hypertension domain. Once PROTÉGÉ generates a knowledge-editing tool based on this task model, then application specialists can enter the *extensions* to the model that define individual treatment plans. The problems of building a task model and of extending that model are therefore separated.

In addition to the form for PLANNING ENTITIES in Figure 7, PROTÉGÉ contains eleven other forms that knowledge engineers fill in to describe various aspects of a task model [Musen 1989a]. Each form acquires information related to a particular topic (attributes of planning entities, properties of attributes of planning entities, actions, attributes of actions, and so on). All the forms contain blanks for making entries, as well as icons that allow transfer from one form to the next. When the user selects with the mouse pointing device a triangular-arrow icon in one of these forms, PROTÉGÉ displays a new form for entry

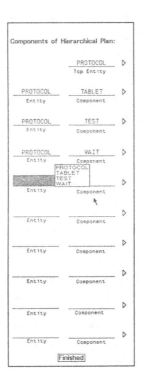

Figure 7. PROTÉGÉ form for planning entities. This form is used to enter the planning entities in an application area and to specify their compositional hierarchy. The knowledge engineer types in the names of the entities using the right column. Before the engineer can type in the name of a new entity, however, he must first identify the "parent" entity of which the new entity is a component. In the hypertension-therapy domain, PROTOCOLS comprise the administration of TABLETs, TESTs, and WAIT periods. Selecting the arrow next to the blank filled in with the word TABLET would open the PROTÉGÉ form in Figure 8.

of information at the next lower level of detail. For example, if the knowledge engineer selects the arrow next to the blank for the TABLET planning entity in Figure 7, PROTÉGÉ will open up a form for editing the *attributes* of TABLETs (Figure 8). PROTÉGÉ uses just one form to solicit the attributes of all planning entities that the knowledge engineer may define. Because different entities necessarily have different attributes, however, the way that the knowledge engineer *fills out* the form will depend on the particular entity the attributes of which are to be entered. When the knowledge engineer selects an arrow next to one of the attributes listed in Figure 8, another PROTÉGÉ form appears for editing the *properties* of the indicated attribute. Thus, PROTÉGÉ uses a hierarchy of graphical forms that acquire knowledge at increasingly fine levels of granularity. All forms in the system permit the user to return to the more general form from which the current form was invoked by selecting an icon labeled *finished*.

Whenever possible, PROTÉGÉ allows the user to fill in the necessary blanks by making selections from pop-up menus that the system generates dynamically. This approach not only minimizes the amount of typing that is necessary, but also helps to ensure that the

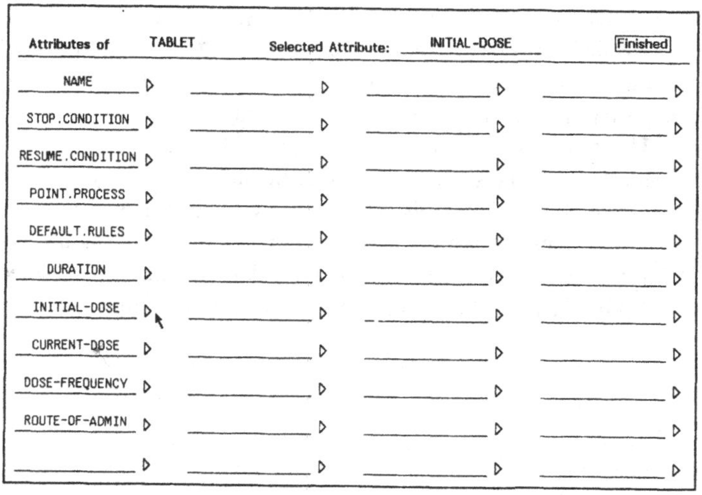

Figure 8. PROTÉGÉ form for attributes of planning entities. This form lists the attributes of the selected class of planning entity—in this case, *tablet*. PROTÉGÉ enters the first six attributes automatically, as these are common to all classes. The knowledge engineer types in the remainder of the attributes. Selecting one of the arrows causes PROTÉGÉ to display another form that describes the properties of the corresponding attribute.

knowledge engineer's entries are consistent with information that has been stipulated previously. The specifications that the user enters into PROTÉGÉ are stored as *n*-tuples in a relational database. When the user selects *invoke editor* from the PROTÉGÉ main menu (see Figure 6), the system queries the database and constructs a knowledge-acquisition tool based on those data that is tailored for the intended application area.

The semantics both of the knowledge engineer's entries into PROTÉGÉ and of the relational-database schema are grounded in the system's predefined model of skeletal-plan refinement. Thus, when a user indicates that hypertension protocols comprise the administration of tablets, tests, and wait periods (as in Figure 7), the intention of these compositional relationships is established by the meaning ascribed to relationships among plan components in the model of skeletal planning. In interacting with PROTÉGÉ, a knowledge engineer consequently uses his understanding of the terms and relationships in the skeletal-planning model to define task-specific concepts in a domain-independent manner.

For each attribute of each task-specific entity that the knowledge engineer describes for PROTÉGÉ (see Figure 8), the engineer must determine how the attribute is associated with a particular distinguishing value and what the data type of that value is. For each such attribute, the knowledge engineer must indicate whether the corresponding value is constant for all instances of that entity. If the value is indeed fixed, then the knowledge engineer simply enters that value into PROTÉGÉ. (For example, the ROUTE-OF-ADMINISTRATION attribute of all instances of antihypertensive tablets has the value *oral*.) If the value varies depending on circumstances that can be determined only at the time that the skeletal plan is refined, then the knowledge engineer indicates to PROTÉGÉ how the target expert system can ascertain that value at run time. (For example, the CURRENT-DOSE attribute of all tablets has an integer value that the target expert system computes via rules that are invoked at the time of each patient consultation.) Alternatively, the value of an attribute may be independent of consultation-related conditions, but contingent on the particular *instance* of the planning entity. (For example, the value of the INITIAL-DOSE attribute of antihypertensive drugs may vary from tablet to tablet, but still may be a constant for any individual tablet instance.) These instance-specific values represent elements of domain knowledge that can be precompiled into the skeletal plans that the target expert system ultimately will refine. The knowledge-acquisition tools that PROTÉGÉ generates allow users to define such instance-specific values for particular application tasks. In entering these values, users of the PROTÉGÉ-generated tools extend the general task model that the knowledge engineer created using PROTÉGÉ, describing individual applications within the task area.

5.2. Custom-Tailored Model-Extending Tools

The knowledge-acquisition tools that PROTÉGÉ creates produce as their output usable knowledge bases. These knowledge bases allow an expert-system shell extracted from the ONCOCIN program (called *e-ONCOCIN*) to solve application tasks via the method of skeletal planning. Users of the PROTÉGÉ-generated knowledge-acquisition tools, however, are not required to think in terms of either the structure of these knowledge bases or the skeletal-planning method. Instead, the users view their interactions in terms of the task model developed using PROTÉGÉ. Like OPAL, the tools generated by PROTÉGÉ help their users to create new knowledge bases by facilitating the extension of task models, and thus are intended for use directly by application specialists [Musen 1989c].

The hypertension-therapy model discussed previously has been used by PROTÉGÉ to create a knowledge editor, *HTN*, that allows physicians to construct knowledge bases for hypertension management [Musen 1989a]. The description of planning entities entered into the PROTÉGÉ form in Figure 7, for example, provides the basis for a graphical environment in HTN in which users depict the procedures for carrying out individual hypertension protocols (Figure 9). The model of skeletal-plan refinement built into PROTÉGÉ assumes that effecting any given plan component necessarily entails carrying out a sequence of operations involving instances of plan components at the next level of granularity. Because the task model entered into PROTÉGÉ states that hypertension protocols comprise the administration of tablets, tests, and wait periods (see Figure 7), the HTN user automatically is presented with a flowchart language for indicating how individual hypertension protocols are composed of a sequence of instances of precisely such elements. The domain-independent icons with which the user represents the flow of control (namely, START, STOP, RANDOMIZE, and DECIDE) and the SUBSCHEMA icon with which he creates graphical subroutines are built into the graphical language; however, the domain-specific icons (namely, TABLET, TEST, and WAIT) are derived from the task model defined at the PROTÉGÉ level. The flowchart shown in Figure 9 describes a typical experimental protocol in which researchers first administer a placebo tablet for three visits, while monitoring the patients' baseline blood pressure. The physicians then prescribe an active antihypertensive drug for several visits, then withhold all medication and observe the patients for any withdrawal effects. Concurrent with this procedure, a number of laboratory investigations are performed at designated intervals.

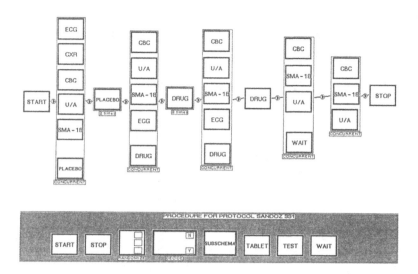

Figure 9. HTN flowchart environment. The HTN knowledge-editing tool includes a graphical language with which physicians draw out the sequence of steps in a protocol for antihypertensive drugs. All task-specific features of this language were derived from the explicit task model that knowledge engineers created previously using PROTÉGÉ. Compare this flowchart with the diagram constructed using OPAL in Figure 4.

When knowledge engineers use PROTÉGÉ to generate knowledge-editing tools for other application areas, similar flowcharting environments are created; the task-dependent aspects of those environments, of course, reflect the models created at the PROTÉGÉ level. Unlike the flowchart language in OPAL, the PROTÉGÉ-generated languages can be modified easily by the knowledge engineer. The developer needs only to edit the task model using PROTÉGÉ and then to regenerate the corresponding knowledge editor. The PROTÉGÉ-derived tools transparently convert the flowchart diagrams that users draw on the workstation screen into augmented transition networks (ATNs) that are incorporated within the knowledge bases of the target expert systems. The e-ONCOCIN inference engine uses these ATNs to determine how instances of skeletal-planning entities (for example, specific hypertension protocols) should be refined into their component skeletal plans from one consultation to the next, Thus, the ATN constructed from the flowchart in Figure 9 would specify that, on the first e-ONCOCIN consultation for a particular patient, the *protocol* should be refined to include the administration of an electrocardiogram (ECG), a chest X-ray study (CXR), a complete blood count (CBC), a urinalysis (U/A), and a blood-chemistry panel (SMA-18)—all of which are instances of *tests*—and that the administration of a placebo *tablet* also should occur. On the occasion of the subsequent consultation for the patient, the ATN would indicate that refinement of the *protocol* plan requires only the administration of *placebo*.

In addition to the flowcharting environments, the tools created by PROTÉGÉ incorporate a variety of graphical forms that are much like those in OPAL (see Figure 3). The domain-specific features of the forms in the PROTÉGÉ-generated system, however, are derived from the explicit task models that knowledge engineers create using PROTÉGÉ. Figure 10, for example, shows one of the graphical forms in HTN. This form allows hypertension

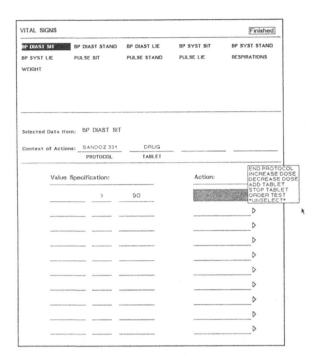

Figure 10. HTN form for vital-sign measurements. This form allows physician experts to enter actions to take within hypertension protocols in response to changes in a patient's vital signs. Here, the expert is about to specify actions for e-ONCOCIN to recommend whenever the treating physician notes that a patient's diastolic blood presure (when measured with the patient in the sitting position) is greater than 90 mm Hg. All task-specific features of this form were derived from the explicit task model created at the PROTÉGÉ level. Compare with the OPAL form in Figure 3. (SYST stands for *systolic*; DIAST stands for *diastolic*; STAND, SIT, and LIE indicate whether the patient is standing, sitting, or lying down when the corresponding measurement is taken.)

specialists to indicate how therapy should be modified in response to changes in a patient's vital signs. A list of possible vital-sign measurements that knowledge engineers previously entered into PROTÉGÉ appears at the top of this form. The HTN form in Figure 10 allows physician-experts to indicate actions that e-ONCOCIN should recommend if the end user notes that any of a patient's vital signs (blood pressure, pulse, weight, or respiratory rate) is elevated, depressed, or within a particular range. In the figure, the expert is about to enter the specification that, if a patient's diastolic blood pressure (measured with the patient in the sitting position) is greater than 90 mm Hg, then the dose of the drug that the patient is taking should be increased. (The expert indicates by how much to increase the dose using another form that HTN subsequently displays.) The menu of permitted actions shown in Figure 10 includes choices such as *end protocol*, *add tablet*, and *order test*. When knowledge engineers created the hypertension task model, the meanings of these actions were specified. Although the hypertension-related actions are relatively simple, in domains such as cancer chemotherapy, task actions can be quite complex and can affect a variety of plan components simultaneously [Musen 1989a]. An application specialist who enters knowledge into a

PROTÉGÉ-generated tool does not need to be concerned with the often-thorny issues of working out the semantics of such actions; the user merely selects the predefined actions from the menu. The user, however, still must understand and agree to the semantics established by the developers who created the relevant task model in the first place.

5.3. The Performance Element: e-ONCOCIN

The e-ONCOCIN shell has been derived from the ONCOCIN cancer-chemotherapy advice system [Tu, et al. 1989] in much the same way that EMYCIN was distilled from the MYCIN program [Buchanan and Shortliffe 1984]. The shell comprises (1) an inference mechanism that instantiates frame hierarchies using methods such as production rules, ATNs, attached procedures, and queries to the expert-system user, (2) a database for storing time-dependent information that was either entered by the end user or concluded by the system during previous consultations [Kahn, Ferguson, Shortliffe, and Fagan 1986], and (3) a graphical user interface that acquires data from the user and that displays the recommendations concluded by the system. The systems created by PROTÉGÉ therefore must deliver to e-ONCOCIN (1) a knowledge base, (2) a database schema, and (3) specifications for constructing the user interface. These three functional components are encoded as a set of objects in an object-oriented programming language [Lane 1986]. Representation of the simple hypertension protocol described in Section 5.2 (see Figures 9 and 10) required HTN to generate 177 objects.

Users interact with e-ONCOCIN much as they do with the original ONCOCIN system [Lane, et al. 1986]. Each time that a consultation is run on a particular case, the user enters data into a time-oriented spreadsheet (Figure 11). Because the complete spreadsheet is typically too large to be displayed on the workstation screen in its entirety, the interface is divided into sections, such that each section refers to a specific class of input data or to a different portion of e-ONCOCIN's recommendation. With the mouse, users select specific sections of the spreadsheet to examine and then enter current input data into the rightmost column of the indicated sections. (The interface makes it convenient for the users to examine data from previous consultations and to review the recommendations that e-ONCOCIN suggested during these past encounters, because the data are displayed chronologically by column.) After all the current data have been entered, e-ONCOCIN completes its refinement of the relevant skeletal plan and displays the system's recommendation in the corresponding portion of the spreadsheet. In Figure 11, the recommendation appears in the sections labeled *tablets* and *tests*.

The e-ONCOCIN system, like any expert-system shell, assumes a particular knowledge-representation syntax (namely, a hierarchy of frames with attached productions rules and ATNs). The semantics of e-ONCOCIN knowledge bases are determined operationally by the behavior that results when the inference engine is applied to those frames, production rules, and ATNs. At the same time, e-ONCOCIN's behavior can be described in terms of the skeletal-planning model that is built into PROTÉGÉ. When a PROTÉGÉ-generated tool is used to build an e-ONCOCIN knowledge base, the tool automatically constructs the frames and other symbols that will cause e-ONCOCIN's activity during a consultation to match the task model that the knowledge engineer first created with PROTÉGÉ and that the application specialist extended using the resultant tool.

Vital Signs	BP SYST LIE							
	BP SYST SIT	150	156	155	154	140	138	125
	BP SYST STAND							
	BP DIAST LIE							
	BP DIAST SIT	100	105	103	103	95	92	85
	BP DIAST STAND							
	PULSE LIE							
	PULSE SIT							
	PULSE STAND							
	RESPIRATIONS							
	WEIGHT							
Tablets	TABLET	PLACEBO	PLACEBO	PLACEBO				
	DOSE TO GIVE	1	1	1				
	DOSE FREQUENCY	BID	BID	BID				
	TIME BETWEEN VISITS	7	7	7				
	TABLET				DRUG	DRUG	DRUG	DRUG
	DOSE TO GIVE				1	2	3	3
	DOSE FREQUENCY				BID	BID	BID	BID
	TIME BETWEEN VISITS				14	14	14	14
Tests	TEST	ECG			ECG			ECG
	TEST	CXR						
	TEST	CBC			CBC			CBC
	TEST	U/A			U/A			U/A
	TEST	SMA-18			SMA-18			SMA-18
	Urinalysis							
	Hematology							
	Adverse Reaction							
	Chemistry							
Time	Day	12	19	26	2	16	30	13
	Month	Jul	Jul	Jul	Aug	Aug	Aug	Sep
	Year	87	87	87	87	87	87	87

Figure 11. Interface for e-ONCOCIN expert systems. In addition to a knowledge base describing a particular hypertension protocol, HTN generates a user interface for e-ONCOCIN based both on the general task model entered into PROTÉGÉ and on the specific hypertension protocol entered into HTN. The interface consists of a spreadsheet, with each column representing the occurrence of a different e-ONCOCIN consultation regarding the same patient case. In the figure, the sequence of tablets and tests that have been administered corresponds with the HTN flowchart diagram in Figure 9.

The model of skeletal planning that knowledge engineers extend at the PROTÉGÉ level to create new task models ultimately is constrained by the limitations of the e-ONCOCIN shell. Thus, a plan described with PROTÉGÉ can be refined only in a top-down manner, because the current e-ONCOCIN architecture does not include a general mechanism for performing backtracking to satisfy constraints [Tu, et al. 1989]. Similarly, the input data described at the PROTÉGÉ level must be associated with only discrete time intervals that correspond with elements of past or current plans—a restriction that reflects the semantics of the e-ONCOCIN temporal data model [Kahn, Ferguson, et al. 1986]. Future work in our laboratory to enhance the capabilities of the e-ONCOCIN shell ultimately will allow refinement of the problem-solving model built into PROTÉGÉ and will expand the applicability of the system. In the absence of a *meta*-metalevel editor to alter PROTÉGÉ's method-specific assumptions, such changes will require manual reprogramming.

6. Discussion

For over 20 years, many workers in AI have viewed knowledge acquisition as a problem in the transfer of expertise. Concentrating on the issue of knowledge transfer, these researchers have tried to identify impediments to successful knowledge acquisition and have suggested that automated tools can help to improve knowledge flow. Historically, the knowledge engineer is perceived as an intermediary who must interview the expert and then transform the expert's rules of thumb into representations that can be interpreted by the computer. Because the knowledge engineer is inexperienced in the application area and because the expert is unable to envision how his knowledge might be captured within the knowledge base, failures in communication are inevitable. In the traditional view, the knowledge-acquisition bottleneck occurs because of these communication difficulties; if the application experts could somehow record their knowledge directly, without having to explain everything to the knowledge engineers, the development and maintenance of knowledge bases would be accelerated.

From the time of TEIRESIAS, the knowledge-acquisition community has struggled to build tools that might allow application specialists to work alone, bypassing the need for knowledge engineers. Although the knowledge-base–maintenance features of TEIRESIAS were never put into practical use, the program set a standard for how most researchers believed automated knowledge-acquisition tools should function. At conferences and in the literature, developers of new tools boast whenever application specialists have been successful in encoding portions of their knowledge without assistance from human intermediaries. Although such examples are laudable, what often is missing from these reports is careful evaluation of the results that have been achieved. It is often impossible to know how to assign credit for a tool's apparent success. What features of the tool, of the application specialist, or of the situations in which the tool was used were most relevant? More important, knowledge entered directly by application specialists themselves is unlikely to be *authentic* (see Section 2.2). Whenever domain experts use knowledge-acquisition tools without the mediating influence of a knowledge engineer, system builders must be willing to accept that the entered knowledge may not reflect the behavior that the experts actually exhibit in practice. Whether the discrepancy significantly degrades the performance of the target expert system almost never is assessed.

OPAL, for example, is a tool that cancer specialists often use alone without the aid of knowledge engineers. Like most knowledge-acquisition programs, there are many aspects of OPAL that never have been evaluated formally. Once the system was put into routine use, however, the obvious rapidity with which oncology protocols could be encoded using OPAL made knowledge engineers unenthusiastic, to say the least, about engaging in academic experiments that required manual knowledge-engineering techniques. At the same time, because the knowledge that users entered into OPAL was never tacit (but rather entailed content knowledge about the doses of drugs and the sequencing of chemotherapies), system builders never saw the need to question the authenticity of the physicians' specifications. Indeed, knowledge bases created with OPAL have been shown to achieve expert-level performance [Shwe, et al. 1989].

The acquisition of authentic knowledge becomes an issue when system builders create new task models. It is during this early stage of knowledge acquisition that developers formulate their initial theories of how experts solve problems. It is also during this early stage that knowledge engineers—and computer-based tools—can greatly facilitate the modeling process.

Many workers in AI have described expert-system knowledge bases as unstructured collections of rules that correspond with the problem-solving heuristics actually used by experts. In this traditional view, the rules are considered to be modular and independent; each rule thus lacks relationships with other rules in the knowledge base and is devoid of any preordained role in problem solving. Recently, however, the elucidation of heuristic classification [Clancey 1985] and of other problem-solving methods [Chandrasekaran 1986; McDermott 1988] has provided an alternative perspective that offers much more guidance to the programmers who develop and maintain complex knowledge bases. In this new light, expert-system behavior need not be caused by the seemingly random results of one "modular" rule triggering the invocation of another; rather, such behavior can result from the application of coherent, domain-independent strategies. Emphasizing these problem-solving methods allows sytem builders to clarify the roles that elicited knowledge plays in arriving at a task solution and provides a structure by which to direct further knowledge-elicitation work. The use of an explicit model of problem solving (such as that of heuristic classification) when creating the incipient task model in no way guarantees that knowledge engineers will obtain authentic knowledge from application specialists. The model's framework simply helps system builders to structure the elicited knowledge and to determine where there still may be gaps.

Models of problem-solving methods vary in the assumptions that they make about the tasks to which the method can be applied. Very general methods, such as heuristic classification, make few assumptions and, therefore, have tremendous applicability. A great many diagnostic tasks and plan-selection operations, for example, can be represented as extensions of the heuristic-classification model. The generality of the model, however, limits the structure that the heuristic-classification model can impose on the way that knowledge engineers represent domain tasks. There is a direct tradeoff between the applicability of a problem-solving model and the guidance that the model can provide for system builders. The more specialized, less widely applicable models incorporated within programs such as MOLE [Eshelman 1988] and SALT [Marcus 1988] have, in practice, been more helpful to developers attempting to structure domain tasks than have more abstract models such as heuristic classification. The advantage of the more specialized models is that they provide greater assistance in distinguishing the different ways in which a problem solver may use domain knowledge to arrive at a solution. To apply these more detailed models, however, system builders must be able to foresee whether a proposed method will be successful in addressing the task at hand, or whether that method will prove to be too restrictive.

Models of problem solving, when embodied within a computer-based tool, are much more useful to system developers than are models that are mapped out only on paper. The ability to translate a user's extensions of the model into machine-readable knowledge bases is an obvious advantage. A more subtle, but perhaps more important, benefit arises because automated tools can facilitate the presentation of complex systems. The graphical forms in PROTÉGÉ, for example, group together related data and emphasize the relationships entered by the user. Each transition from one form to another moves the user's view of the task model that he is creating to a different level within an abstraction hierarchy. The forms help to break up a knowledge engineer's entries into manageable portions, and the relationships among the forms emphasize the relationships among the components of the user's specifications. The same advantages in knowledge presentation accrue in model-extending tools as well. Users of programs such as OPAL and those generated by PROTÉGÉ benefit from graphical presentation formats that accentuate the relationships among large numbers of entries and that organize those entries coherently.

PROTÉGÉ offers the additional advantage that users can extend a predefined model of problem solving in two discrete stages. Knowledge engineers first extend a model of skeletal-plan refinement to create a task model. Domain experts then extend that task model (itself an extension of the model of the method) to define individual applications. By viewing knowledge acquisition as the process of task-model formation followed by the process of task-model extension, system builders can think critically about these two phases of the expert-system lifecycle and can identify features of knowledge-acquisition tools best suited for each phase. Rather than concentrating on whether the need for knowledge engineers has been obviated by a particular tool—and implicitly assuming that eliminating the knowledge engineers is a necessary and sufficient metric of success—developers can consider the *roles* that knowledge engineers might play in helping application specialists to build models. The knowledge engineer should be regarded as a potential partner, rather than as an inherent marplot, allowing workers in AI to develop more effective strategies for acquiring and representing the tacit knowledge that separates experts from novices. At the same time, by recognizing the ease with which application specialists can enter the content knowledge that extends pre-existing models, developers can build tools such as OPAL that experts can indeed use independently.

The PROTÉGÉ system demonstrates a divide-and-conquer strategy that separates the model-building work that application specialists best perform with the aid of knowledge engineers from the model-extending work that application specialists easily can perform independently. At the PROTÉGÉ level, knowledge engineers work with domain experts to build models of tasks that can be solved using the method of skeletal-plan refinement. These models can then be used as the foundation for custom-tailored knowledge-editing tools. PROTÉGÉ is used to map out the structure of the task and, consequently, the *process* by which a problem solver might arrive at a recommendation. The tools that PROTÉGÉ generates, on the other hand, acquire knowledge about the *content* of specific plans. Although these two phases of knowledge acquisition sometimes may be strictly sequential in nature, attempts to enter content knowledge frequently point out deficiencies in the initial task model; PROTÉGÉ's division of labor allows knowledge engineers to alter the task model easily whenever application specialists encounter problems during their model-extension work. (With OPAL, changes to the task model always required cumbersome reprogramming of LISP code.)

The decision regarding the optimum way to separate task knowledge into a fixed, reusable portion and a variable, application-specific portion is an important judgment that all PROTÉGÉ users must face. The declaration of the classes of entities in the domain and the attributes of those entities is necessarily part of the task model entered into PROTÉGÉ. The values of those attributes, however, may either be predefined as part of the task model (or have predefined methods by which the attributes' values may be concluded) or be identified as content knowledge to be entered by the user of the tool that PROTÉGÉ generates.

Whether an attribute's value should be considered a constant element of the task model or part of the application-specific content knowledge is determined by the nature of the task domain and by the role that that attribute plays in problem solving.

Although demonstrated within the context of the skeletal-planning method, the PROTÉGÉ approach also should apply to other methods of problem solving. For example, if the system were adapted for an inference engine that is well-suited for solving problems using heuristic classification (such as EMYCIN), knowledge engineers then would use PROTÉGÉ to create models of classification tasks, rather than models of planning tasks. A knowledge engineer, for instance, might use PROTÉGÉ to describe the set of classification problems that is encountered during geological mineral exploration, as was done in the Prospector system [Reboh 1981]. A knowledge-acquisition tool generated by PROTÉGÉ then could be used by expert geologists to enter specific ore-deposit models. The ore-deposit models could be converted to knowledge bases for expert systems that workers in the field would use to detemine the most favorable drilling sites for particular minerals.

Where there are multiple, related tasks within an application area—and when there is thus the need to construct multiple knowledge bases—the PROTÉGÉ approach offers a considerable advantage. The difficult problem of creating a computational model of the domain task does not disappear; the need for knowledge engineers to help application specialists to build such a model does not disappear either. Nevertheless, the methodology allows system builders to confront only a single bottleneck. If knowledge engineers and domain experts first use tools such as PROTÉGÉ to build the required task models, those experts then can go to work on their own, extending those task models to define multiple knowledge bases. The models incorporated within the tools that PROTÉGÉ generates, however, may not always account for all the professional behaviors that system builders ultimately may observe in an application area. When the user of a PROTÉGÉ-generated tool is unable to extend the given task model to specify a required action (that is, if he must unexpectedly describe an entity that is not within the original model), the task model may have to be augmented at the PROTÉGÉ level.

Like natural theories that are proposed, tested, and revised, the models constructed by knowledge-acquisition tools display a distinct life cycle. Workers in AI have built a variety of tools, each addressing different aspects of this modeling process. Tools such as ROGET assist developers with the initial model-building phase when the task still may be ill defined. Tools such as OPAL aid in the final model-extending phase, when the task area is well understood and end users require multiple, related knowledge bases. The new challenge is to integrate these approaches, allowing model building to be followed by model extension, providing continuous assistance from the time that the application task is first identified to the time that the final knowledge base is disseminated to end users.

PROTÉGÉ is the first step toward that integration. Workers in AI, however, have not yet identified an optimal technology for acquiring knowledge for expert systems, and even less is known about acquiring domain knowledge for the purposes of building *knowledge-acquisition tools*. Consequently, there will be substantial opportunities for research as the PROTÉGÉ approach is broadened to other task areas, to other problem-solving methods, and to other knowledge-system architectures. In the process of expanding the techniques demonstrated by PROTÉGÉ, we shall be able to learn more about the structure and applicability of new problem-solving methods and about the modeling of domain tasks.

Acknowledgments

Development of OPAL and PROTÉGÉ was supported in part by grants LM-07033 and LM-04420 from the National Library of Medicine. Computing facilities were provided by the SUMEX-AIM resource under NIH grant RR-00785. Lyn Dupré, Tom Gruber, and Sandra Marcus provided valuable comments on an earlier draft of this paper.

Notes

1. We also could refer to each situation in which the model applies as an *instantiation*, although many authors reserve that word for descriptions of symbols within a knowledge-representation language. In this paper, therefore, I use the term *extension*.

References

Addis, T.R. 1987. A framework for knowledge elicitation. In *Proceedings of the First European Workshop on Knowledge Acquisition for Knowledge-Based Systems*, Reading University, Reading, England.

Anderson, J.R. 1987. Skill acquisition: Compilation of weak-method problem solutions. *Psychological Review*, 94: 192–210.

Belkin, N.J., Brooks, H.M., and Daniels, P.J. 1987. Knowledge elicitation using discourse analysis. *International Journal of Man–Machine Studies*, 27: 127–144.

Bennett, J.S. 1985. ROGET: A knowledge-based system for acquiring the conceptual structure of a diagnostic expert system. *Journal of Automated Reasoning*, 1: 49–74.

Boose 1989. A survey of knowledge acquisition techniques and tools. *Knowledge Acquisition*, 1: 3–37.

Breuker, J., and Wielinga, B. 1987. Use of models in the interpretation of verbal data. In A.L. Kidd (Ed.), *Knowledge acquisition for expert systems: A practical handbook*. London: Plenum.

Buchanan, B.G., and Shortliffe, E.H. 1984. *Rule-based expert systems: The MYCIN experiments of the Stanford heuristic programming project*. Reading, MA: Addison-Wesley.

Chandrasekaran, B. 1986. Generic tasks for knowledge-based reasoning: High-level building blocks for expert system design. *IEEE Expert*, 1: 23–30.

Clancey, W.J. 1985. Heuristic classification. *Artificial Intelligence*, 27: 289–350.

Clancey, W.J. 1986. Viewing knowledge bases as qualitative models. (Technical Report KSL-86-27). Stanford, CA: Knowledge Systems Laboratory, Stanford University.

Cleaves, D.A. 1987. Cognitive biases and corrective techniques: Proposals for improving elicitation procedures for knowledge-based systems. *International Journal of Man–Machine Studies*, 27: 155–166.

Conklin, J. 1987. Hypertext: An introduction and survey. *Computer*, 20: 17–41.

Cooke, N.M., and McDonald, J.E. 1987. The application of psychological scaling techniques to knowledge elicitation for knowledge-based systems. *International Journal of Man–Machine Studies*, 26: 533–550.

Davis, R. 1976. *Applications of Meta Level Knowledge to the Construction, Maintenance, and Use of Large Knowledge Bases*. Ph.D. thesis, Technical Report STAN-CS-76-564, Stanford University, Stanford, CA.

Ericsson, K.A., and Simon, H.A. 1984. *Protocol analysis: Verbal reports as data*. Cambridge, MA: MIT Press.

Eshelman, L. 1988. MOLE: A knowledge-acquisition system for cover-and-differentiate systems. In S. Marcus (Ed.), *Automating knowledge acquisition for expert systems*. Boston: Kluwer Academic Publishers.

Fitts, P.M. 1964. Perceptual-motor skill learning. In A. Melton (Ed.), *Categories of human learning*. New York: Academic Press.

Fodor, J.A. 1968. The appeal of tacit knowledge in psychological explanation. *Journal of Philosophy*, 65: 627–640.

Friedland, P.E. 1969. *Knowledge-Based Experiment Design in Molecular Genetics*. Ph.D. thesis, Technical Report STAN-CS-79-771, Stanford University, Stanford, CA.

Friedland, P.E., and Iwasaki, Y. 1985. The concept and implementation of skeletal plans. *Journal of Automated Reasoning*, *1*: 161–208.

Freiling, M.J., and Alexander, J.H. 1984. Diagrams and grammars: Tools for mass producing expert systems. In *The First Conference on Artificial Intelligence Applications* (pp. 537–543). Denver, CO: IEEE Computer Society Press.

Gale, W.A. 1987. Knowledge-based knowledge acquisition for a statistical consulting system. *International Journal of Man-Machine Studies*, *13*: 81–116.

Johnson, P.E. 1983. What kind of expert should a system be? *Journal of Medicine and Philosophy*, 8: 77–97.

Kahn, G., Nowlan, S., and McDermott, J. 1985. Strategies for knowledge acquisition. *IEEE Transactions on Pattern Analysis and Machine Intelligence*, *PAMI-7*: 511–522.

Kahn, M.G., Ferguson, J.C., Shortliffe, E.H., and Fagan, L.M. 1985. Representation and use of temporal information in ONCOCIN. In *Proceedings of the Ninth Annual Symposium on Computer Applications in Medical Care*. Baltimore, MD: IEEE Computer Society Press.

Kitto, C.M. 1989. Progress in automated knowledge acquisition tools: How close are we to replacing the knowledge engineer? *Knowledge Acquisition*, in press.

Klinker, G. 1988. KNACK: Sample-driven knowledge acquisition for reporting systems. In S. Marcus (Ed.), *Automating knowledge acquisition for expert systems*. Boston: Kluwer Academic Publishers.

LaBerge, D., and Samuels, S.J. 1974. Toward a theory of automatic information processing in reading. *Cognitive Psychology*, *6*: 293–323.

Lane, C.D. 1986. *Ozone reference manual*. (Technical Report KSL-86-40). Stanford, CA: Knowledge Systems Laboratory, Stanford University.

Lane, C.D., Walton, J.D., and Shortliffe, E.H. 1986. Graphical access to medical expert systems: II. Design of an interface for physicians. *Methods of Information in Medicine*, *25*: 143–150.

Lyons, W. 1986. *The disappearance of introspection*. Cambridge, MA: MIT Press.

Marcus, S. 1988. SALT: A knowledge acquisition tool for propose-and-revise systems. In S. Marcus (Ed.), *Automating knowledge acquisition for expert systems*. Boston: Kluwer Academic Publishers.

McCarthy, J. 1968. Programs with common sense. In M. Minsky (Ed.), *Semantic information processing*, Cambridge, MA: MIT Press.

McDermott, J. 1988. Preliminary steps toward a taxonomy of problem-solving methods. In S. Marcus (Ed.), *Automating knowledge acquisition for expert systems*. Boston: Kluwer Academic Publishers.

Meyer, M.A., Mniszewski, S.M., and Peaslee, A. 1989. Use of three minimally-biasing elicitation techniques for knowledge acquisition. *Knowledge Acquisition*, 1: 59–71.

Michalski, R.S., and Chilausky, R.L. 1980. Knowledge acquisition by encoding expert rules versus computer induction from examples: A case study involving soybean pathology. *International Journal of Man–Machine Studies*, *12*: 63–87.

Musen, M.A., Fagan, L.M., Combs, D.M., and Shortliffe, E.H. 1987. Use of a domain model to drive an interactive knowledge-editing tool. *International Journal of Man-Machine Studies*, *26*: 105–121.

Musen, M.A., Fagan, L.M., and Shortliffe, E.H. 1988. Graphical specification of procedural knowledge for an expert system. In J. Hendler (Ed.), *Expert systems: The user interface*. Norwood, NJ: Ablex.

Musen, M.A. 1989a. *Automated generation of model-based knowledge-acquisition tools*. London: Pitman.

Musen, M.A. 1989b. An editor for the conceptual models of interactive knowledge-acquisition tools. *International Journal of Man-Machine Studies*, in press.

Musen, M.A. 1989c. Conceptual models of interactive knowledge-acquisition tools. *Knowledge Acquisition*, 1: 73–88.

Newell, A. 1982. The knowledge level. *Artificial Intelligence*, *18*: 87–127.

Nisbett, R.E., and Wilson, T.D. 1977. Telling more than we can know: Verbal reports on mental processes. *Psychological review*, *84*: 231–259.

Reboh, R. 1981. *Knowledge engineering techniques and tools in the Prospector environment*. (Technical Report 243). Menlo Park, CA: SRI International.

Regoczei, S., and Plantinga, E.P.O. 1987. Creating the domain of discourse: Ontology and inventory. *International Journal of Man-Machine Studies*, *27*: 235–250.

Rumelhart, D.E., and Norman, D.A. 1983. *Representation in memory*. (Technical Report CHIP 116). San Diego, La Jolla, CA: Center for Human Information Processing, University of California.

Silverman, H.A. 1975. *A digitalis therapy advisor*. (Technical Report MAC/TR-143). Cambridge, MA: Massachusetts Institute of Technology.

Slovic, P., and Lichtenstein, S. 1971. Comparison of Bayesian and regression approaches to the study of information processing in judgment. *Organizational Behavior and Human Performance*, 6: 649–744.

Shwe, M.A., Tu, S.W., and Fagan, L.M. 1989. Validating the knowledge base of a therapy-planning system. *Methods of Information in Medicine*, 28: 36–50.

Swartout, W.R. 1981. *Producing Explanations and Justifications of Expert Consulting Programs*, Ph.D. thesis, Technical Report MIT/LCS/TR-251, Massachusetts Institute of Technology.

Tu, S.W., Kahn, M.G., Musen, M.A., Ferguson, J.C., Shortliffe, E.H., and Fagan, L.M. 1989. Episodic monitoring of time-oriented data for heuristic skeletal-plan refinement. *Communications of the ACM*, in press.

Winograd, T., and Flores, F. 1986. *Understanding Computers and Cognition: A New Foundation for Design*. Norwood, NJ: Ablex.

Machine Learning, 4, 377–394 (1989)

Knowledge Acquisition for Knowledge-Based Systems: Notes on the State-of-the-Art

JOHN H. BOOSE
Advanced Technology Center, Boeing Computer Services, 7L-64, PO Box 24346, Seattle, Washington, 98124, USA

BRIAN R. GAINES
Department of Computer Science, University of Calgary, 2500 University Dr. NW, Calgary, Alberta, Canada T2N 1N4

Abstract. Notes from the organizers of a series of knowledge acquisition workshops are presented here. The state-of-the-art in knowledge acquisition research is briefly described. Then the technology of interactive knowledge acquisition is discussed, including a descriptive framework, dimensions of use, and research patterns. Finally, dissemination of information from knowledge acquisition workshops is detailed.

Key Words: knowledge acquisition, knowledge acquisition tools, knowledge acquisition methods, knowledge-based systems, expertise transfer, knowledge elicitation.

1. Knowledge Acquisition—State-of-the-Art

At the time of the first AAAI Sponsored Workshop on Knowledge Acquisition for Knowledge-Based Systems in Banff, November 1986, the literature on knowledge acquisition was sparse, scattered in conference publications, and difficult to access. The 1986 Workshop and the ensuing journal publication of some forty papers representing the state-of-the-art world-wide changed that situation. The inclusion of sessions on knowledge acquisition in many conferences, the European Workshops on Knowledge Acquisition for Knowledge-Based Systems in London and Reading, September 1987, Bonn in June 1988 and Paris in July 1989, the Banff Workshops in October 1987, November 1988 and October 1989, and the establishment of a new knowledge acquisition journal (see below) have changed the situation even further. We now have a worldwide network of communicating researchers aware of one another's activities and an open, widely disseminated and readily available literature on knowledge acquisition.

The problem now is not so much to access research and experience in knowledge acquisition, but to make sense of the diverse and wide-ranging material available and, in particular, to apply the results to improve effectiveness in the development of knowledge-based systems. There are major impediments to such understanding and application:

— A diversity of techniques and tools that overlap in their applications but that may be either competitive alternatives or complementary partners
— Lack of variety, detail, and evaluation in the case histories of applications of the techniques and tools

131

— Lack of access to the techniques and tools outside the narrow research communities originating them
— Lack of standardization in the knowledge representation resulting from the techniques and tools, making it difficult to integrate them and to interface them to existing knowledge-based systems
— Lack of standardization in the forms of data required by the techniques and tools making it difficult to apply them in the same situation and compare them
— Lack of standardization in the user interfaces to the interactive tools making it difficult to integrate them in an effective environment for human-computer interaction
— Lack of portability in the run-time environments required by the tools making it difficult to integrate them with other systems

These are not unreasonable problems at this stage of development of knowledge-based systems. We are in the midst not only of the evolution of a rapidly developing technology but a revolution of our understanding of the nature of knowledge and knowledge processes in society and technology. Premature standardization resulting in over-rigid systems would be inappropriate and a major impediment to progress. However, we have to balance the need for integration, dissemination, and application of knowledge acquisition techniques and tools against the dangers of rigidity.

1.1. Knowledge Acquisition in Context: Knowledge-Based System Technologies

Knowledge acquisition can be considered as one further technology contributing to the development of knowledge-based systems (KBS). Figure 1 places it in the context of the related technologies which make up the virtual machine hierarchy of existing KBS.

— **Knowledge Support System:** at the top of the hierarchy are experimental systems integrating knowledge acquisition and performance tools in systems designed to support knowledge base updating and extension as part of ongoing applications.
— **Knowledge Acquisition Tools:** at the next level are the tools for automating knowledge engineering for KBS, through automatic interview procedures, modeling expert behavior, and analysis of knowledge in textual form.
— **Knowledge-Based System Support Environment:** at the third level of the hierarchy is the equivalent of the Application Programming Support Environment (APSE) in conventional systems, with facilities for editing, displaying, debugging, and validating the knowledge base.
— **Knowledge-Based System Shell:** at the fourth level of the hierarchy is the knowledge-based system shell as a run-time environment that elicits problem-specific information from the user, provides advice based on its knowledge base, and explains that advice in as much detail as required.
— **Shell Development Language:** at the fifth level of the hierarchy is the language in which the knowledge-based system shell is written, generally a special-purpose environment for coping with knowledge representation and inference.

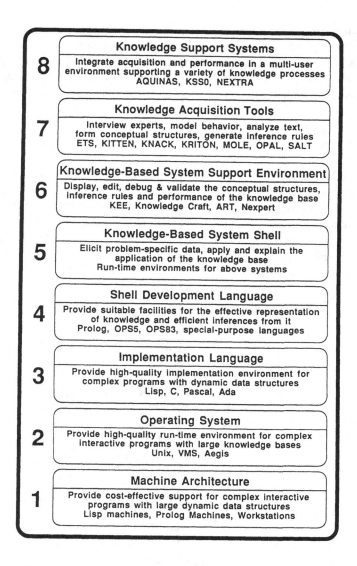

Figure 1. Knowledge-based systems virtual machine hierarchy.

— **Implementation Language:** at the sixth level of the hierarchy is the implementation language which actually interfaces to the computer. This tended to be Lisp in the early days of KBS, but as speed and space efficiency have become significant and knowledge representation has become better understood, other languages that support dynamic data structures such as C and Pascal have become widely used.

— **Operating System:** at the seventh level of the hierarchy is the operating system within which the implementation runs. This needs to provide good interfaces to other programs, large databases and communications.

— **Machine Architecture:** at the lowest level of the hierarchy is the machine on which the KBS runs. In theory, system developers should not need to know about the lower levels of the hierarchy-machine architectures, operating systems, and implementation languages are remote from knowledge processing. In practice, these lower levels are the foundations on which systems are built, and any defects in them can undermine the functionality of the upper levels.

1.2. Trends in Knowledge Engineering

The basic model for knowledge engineering has been that the knowledge engineer mediates between the expert and knowledge base, eliciting knowledge from the expert, modeling and encoding it for the knowledge base, and refining it in collaboration with the expert to achieve acceptable performance. Figure 2 shows this basic model with manual acquisition of knowledge from an expert followed by interactive application of the knowledge with multiple clients through an expert system shell.

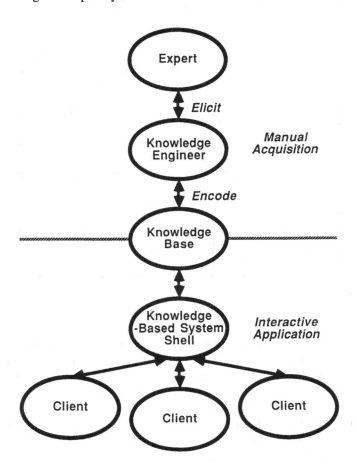

Figure 2. Basic model of manual knowledge acquisition.

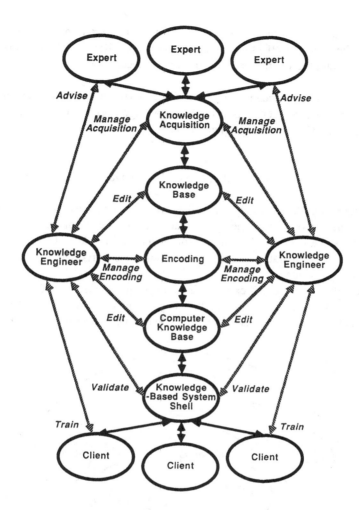

Figure 3. Knowledge engineers' roles in interactive computer-based knowledge acquisition.

This basic model has been greatly extended by the introduction of interactive knowledge acquisition and encoding tools allowing the expert to enter knowledge directly to the system without an intermediary. Such tools can greatly reduce the need for the knowledge engineer to act as an intermediary, but, in most applications, they leave a substantial role for the knowledge engineer.

As shown in Figure 3, knowledge engineers may:

— Advise the expert on the process of interactive knowledge elicitation
— Manage the interactive knowledge acquisition tools, setting them up appropriately
— Edit the partially encoded knowledge base in collaboration with the expert
— Manage the knowledge encoding tools, setting them up appropriately
— Edit the encoded knowledge base in collaboration with the expert

— Validate the application of the knowledge base in collaboration with the expert
— Train the clients in the effective use of the knowledge base in collaboration with the expert by developing operational and training procedures

This use of interactive computer-based elicitation can be combined with manual elicitation and with the use of the interactive tools by the knowledge engineer rather than, or in addition to, the expert. The knowledge engineer can:

— Directly elicit knowledge from the expert
— Use the interactive elicitation tools to enter knowledge into the knowledge base

Figure 3 shows multiple knowledge engineers since the tasks above may require the effort of more than one person, and some specialization may be appropriate. Multiple experts are also shown since it is rare for one person to have all the knowledge required, and, even if this were so, comparative elicitation form multiple experts is itself a valuable knowledge elicitation technique.

Figure 3 also shows the complexity of the knowledge engineer's role and some of the support tools required. Figure 4 groups the support tools for editing, display, encoding, and validation of the knowledge bases into a Knowledge-Based System Support Environment

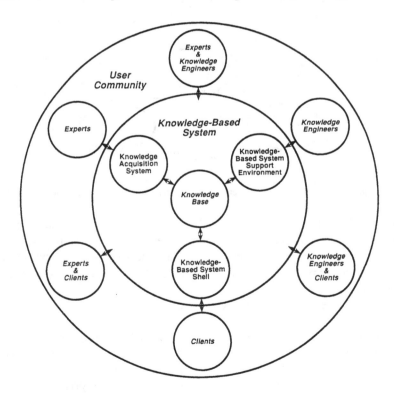

Figure 4. Major components of a knowledge based system.

and combines the various forms of knowledge bases together. It shows the overall structure of a knowledge-based system as a central knowledge base interacting through the knowledge acquisition tools, the expert system support environment, and expert system shell, with a user community of experts, knowledge engineers, and clients.

The next section describes current knowledge acquisition tools and techniques.

2. Knowledge Acquisition Tools and Techniques

At the workshops, papers on knowledge acquisition tools and techniques discussed *manual* methods (for instance, protocol analysis), *automated* tools (traditional machine learning techniques), *interactive* computer-based tools, or combinations of these [Boose, 1989]. This section concentrates on the interactive tools.

One way to classify computer-based interactive knowledge acquisition tools is to associate them with knowledge-based application *problems* and problem-solving *methods*. Many tool developers describe their work in these terms. They feel that examining the roles that knowledge plays or the requirements of problem-solving methods structures tool development. This descriptive approach provides a framework for analyzing and comparing tools and techniques, shows the strengths and weaknesses of a method or tool, and focuses the knowledge acquisition process on the task of building useful knowledge-based systems.

Musen proposed that knowledge acquisition tools could be associated with specific problems or with specific problem-solving methods [Musen, 1987]. In a related manner, we have worked to classify tools with problems *and* problem-solving methods, since most problems are strongly linked to certain types of problem-solving methods. Consequently, certain types of domain knowledge and possibly control knowledge should be acquired to build the corresponding knowledge-based system. This idea was discussed at the First AAAI-Sponsored Knowledge Acquisition for Knowledge-Based Systems Workshop held in Banff, Canada, in November, 1986 [Gaines and Boose, 1989]. Builders of interactive knowledge acquisition tools were asked to classify their research and the research of others in terms of these relationships.

Clancey [1986] introduced two hierarchies, one for application problems and one for problem-solving methods (Figure 5) [Boose, 1989]. Broadly, the problem hierarchy divides into *analysis* (interpretation) and *synthesis* (construction) problems. Generally, analysis problems involve identifying sets of objects based on their features. One typical characteristic of analysis problems is that a complete set of solutions can be enumerated and included in the system. Synthesis (generative or constructive) problems require that a solution be built up from component pieces or subproblem solutions. In synthesis problems there are often too many potential solutions to enumerate and include explicitly in the system.

High-level application problems include identification, prediction, control, design, specification, and modification assembly. Identification is further broken down into diagnosis and monitoring; design is broken down into configuration and planning. Presumably, lower levels in the problem hierarchy would be sub-problems (i.e., troubleshooting and symptom analysis would be found under diagnosis), and the leaves of the problem hierarchy would be specific application problems to be solved.

Problem-solving methods described by Clancey include *heuristic classification* and *heuristic construction*. Relationships exist between problems and these methods. For instance,

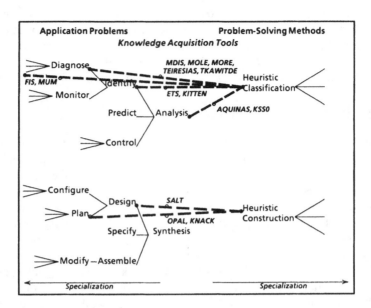

Figure 5. Knowledge acquisition tools may be associated with relationships between application problems and problem-solving methods. Representative tools shown above include are listed below (tools are discussed in more detail in Boose, 1989).

the heuristic classification problem-solving method has been used for many knowledge-based systems that solve analysis problems and is employed in a variety of knowledge-based system development tools, or "shells" (S.1, M.1, EMYCIN, TI-PC, and so on). In heuristic classification, data is abstracted up through a problem hierarchy, problem abstractions are mapped onto solution abstractions, and solution abstractions are refined down through the solution hierarchy into specific solutions.

General methods that have been applied to synthesis problems are sparse; Clancey classified these methods under heuristic construction. Usually, a specific method is developed to solve a particular problem (such as SALT's propose-and-revise method or OPAL's skeletal-plan-refinement method), but it may be difficult to generalize the method. Some form of directed backtracking or cyclic constraint exploration is often used to explore the problem space.

Many problems require a combination of problem-solving methods. For instance, Clancey outlines a maintenance cycle requiring monitoring, prediction, diagnosis, and modification; this would combine aspects of heuristic classification and heuristic construction. Sometimes heuristic construction is used to solve analysis problems, and sometimes heuristic classification is used to structure portions of less complex synthesis problems.

The dashed lines in Figure 5 represent interactive knowledge acquisition tools that are associated with links between problems and problem-solving methods. Some tools are associated with high-level problems (Aquinas, KSS0), some are associated with sub-problem classes (MDIS, MOLE, SALT), and some are associated with specific application systems (FIS, MUM).

Representative tools shown in Figure 5 include:

AQUINAS—elicit and model information using a knowledge acquisition workbench including hierarchically structured repertory grid-based interviewing and testing and other methods [Boose and Bradshaw, 1987b], [Kitto and Boose, 1987], [Boose and Bradshaw, 1987a], [Boose, 1988], [Bradshaw and Boose, 1989], [Kitto and Boose, 1988], [Shema and Boose, 1988], [Boose, Bradshaw, and Shema, 1988]

ETS—interview experts using repertory grid-based methods and test the knowledge [Boose, 1984, 1985, 1986a, b]

FIS—tie knowledge acquisition closely to the fault diagnosis domain [De Jong, 1987]

KITTEN—interview experts using repertory grid-based methods [Shaw and Gaines, 1987], [Shaw and Woodward, 1988]

KNACK—elicit and use knowledge about evaluation report generation [Klinker, Bentolila, Genetet, Grimes, and McDermott, 1987], [Klinker, Genetet, and McDermott, 1988]

KSS0—elicit knowledge with a repertory grid-based interviewing tool including text analysis, behavior induction, and psychological scaling techniques [Gaines, 1987a, 1987b, 1988], [Gaines and Sharp, 1987], [Shaw and Gaines, 1987], [Shaw, 1988]

MDIS—experts are interviewed to describe mechanisms in a top-down structured manner for diagnostic problems [Antonelli, 1983]

MOLE—exploit information about how problems are solved to elicit scarce diagnostic knowledge and use feedback to fine tune the knowledge [Eshelman, Ehret, McDermott, and Tan, 1987], [Eshelman, 1988]

MORE—exploit information about how problems are solved to elicit extensive diagnostic knowledge [Kahn, Nowlan, McDermott, 1985a, b]

MUM—evidential combination knowledge and control knowledge are elicited for medical problems [Gruber and Cohen, 1987]

OPAL—tie knowledge acquisition closely to the cancer treatment domain [Musen, Fagan, Combs, and Shortliffe, 1987]

SALT—elicit and deliver knowledge for constructive constraint satisfaction tasks [Marcus, McDermott, and Wang, 1985], [Marcus, 1987], [Stout, Caplain, Marcus, and McDermott, 1988]

TEIRESIAS—model existing knowledge to monitor refinements and help debug consultations [Davis and Lenat, 1982]

TKAW/TDE—exploit information about how problems are solved to elicit trouble-shooting knowledge [Kahn, Breaux, Joeseph, and DeKlerk, 1987]

Associations between problem domains and problem-solving methods help define the depth and breadth of current knowledge acquisition research. For example, Boeing's research using AQUINAS has led them to try to build a broad link (multiple integrated tool sets) between a general application problem class (analysis problems) and a powerful problem-solving method (heuristic classification). Other successful work has led researchers to tightly couple knowledge acquisition tools to a domain problem (for example FIS, STUDENT, OPAL).

Associations in the problem-method framework where no tools exist can point out promising areas for new research. For example, can special types of knowledge acquisition tools be associated with debugging problems and heuristic classification or with planning and new specializations of heuristic construction?

A more detailed analysis of this classification, description of tools, and research strategies associated with them are contained in [Boose, 1989]. This study also lists manual techniques and automated (machine learning) techniques presented at the workshops and provides a catalog of tools and methods.

2.1. Knowledge Acquisition Tool Dimensions

Diverse interactive computer-based tools have been developed to assist the knowledge acquisition process. To help focus discussion at the first knowledge acquisition workshop, we used AQUINAS to classify the tools and develop tool dimensions. We present the results here to give an impression of similarity and differences among the tools.

Knowledge in AQUINAS is represented, in part, in networks of repertory grids. Objects appear along one axis of a grid and dimensions or traits appear along the other axis. AQUINAS helps the expert develop, analyze, refine, and test knowledge. A grid showing twenty-six interactive knowledge acquisition tools and associated analyses is shown in [Boose, 1989].

AQUINAS elicited the following set of interactive knowledge acquisition tool descriptors:

Application task dimensions

— **Level of generality** (domain dependence)—How domain-dependent is the tool?
— **Analysis/synthesis**—What broad categories of application tasks can the tool address?
— **Specific problem**—Has the tool been built for a specific problem? If so, what is the problem?
— **Application statistics**—(number and size of applications)—How many applications have been built with the tool? How diverse are they? How large are they? How much of the finished system did the tool help build?

Knowledge acquisition techniques and methods—What general knowledge acquisition techniques are employed?

— **Psychology-Based and Interviewing Methods**
  • Automated/Mixed-initiative Interviewing—the tool interviews the expert
  • Protocol analysis (Case Walk-Through/Eidetic Reduction/Observation/Process-Tracing) —record and analyze transcripts from experts thinking aloud during tasks
  • Psychological Scaling (including multidimensional scaling)—use scaling techniques to help structure knowledge
  • Repertory Grids/PCP—use personal construct psychology and related methods to elicit and analyze knowledge
— **Task/Method/Performance Exploitation**
  • Domain Exploitation (Single Application)—rely heavily on the domain for knowledge acquisition guidance
  • Problem-Solving Method Exploitation—use information about the problem-solving method to guide knowledge acquisition

- Performance System (direct link or embedded)—generate knowledge that may be directly tested and used
— **Modeling**
  - Decision Analysis—perform probabilistic inference and planning using influence diagrams
  - Modeling (deep models, causal models, cognitive models, conceptual models, mediating representations, task-level models)—use or generate models of the domain, possibly independent of a tool or a specific application
  - Consistency Analysis—analyze knowledge for consistency
  - Physical Model Simulation—use basic laws to derive physical models through simulation
— **Multiple Experts**
  - Delphi—gather information from people independently
  - Multiple Source—elicit and analyze knowledge from multiple sources separately and combine for use
— **Other Sources of Knowledge**
  - Textual Analysis/Natural Language Analysis—generate knowledge directly by analyzing text Modeling dimensions
— **Deep Modeling/Shallow Modeling**—Are "deep" models or "causal" models elicited?
— **Multiple/Single Methods for Handling Uncertainty**—What techniques, if any, are used to model uncertainty?

Representations

— **Expertise representation method** ("intermediate" representation) (structures, hierarchies, operators, probability distributions, relations, repertory grids, rules, scripts, tables)
— **Knowledge types** (causal knowledge, classes, conceptual structures, constraints, control, covering, example cases, explanations, facts, goals, judgments, justifications, preferences, procedures, relations, spatial, strategic, temporal, terminology, uncertainties)

Features

— **High-level techniques/low-level techniques**—How sophisticated are the techniques used?
— **Learning component** (automatic, interactive, none)—If there is a learning component in the tool, how powerful is it? Is it automatic or interactive?
— **Multiple features/few features**—How many techniques are integrated in a single framework? How well do multiple techniques support each other?
— **Multiple knowledge sources support**—Is there specific support for eliciting, analyzing, or delivering knowledge from multiple experts or other sources?
— **Multiple knowledge views/few knowledge views**—How many ways are there to look at elicited knowledge? What, if any, knowledge transformation techniques are employed?

System use

— **Automated tool/semi-automated tool/manual technique**—How much of the technique is implemented as a computer program? How "smart" is the tool? Is effective tool use dependent on the user, or does the tool offer semi-automated or automated assistance?

— **Efficiency of use; speed of use**—How hard is the tool to use? How efficient is knowledge elicitation and modeling? How well are the techniques implemented?
— **Implementation stage** (planned, in progress, implemented, tested, in use, past use)
— **Intended users** (end-users of expert system, decision makers, experts, knowledge engineers, AI programmers needed)—Who are the targeted users of the tool?
— **Life cycle support** (one-shot use to complete cycle support)—How much of the knowledge engineering and system delivery life cycle does the tool support?
— **System in use/system not in use**—Is the tool currently in use? Was the tool previously in use? Will the tool be in use in the future?
— **Training needed**—How much training is needed to use the tool? Can experts use the tool directly?
— **Validation, verification, maintenance**—Does the tool offer support for testing and maintenance?

AQUINAS performed several analyses of the knowledge. For example, an implication analysis produced by AQUINAS showed logical entailments between different dimensions. A similarity analysis among dimensions showed, for example, that EFFICIENT.AND.-FAST.TO.USE was closely coupled to LITTLE.TRAINING.NEEDED. A similarity analysis among tools showed, for example, high similarity between ETS, KITTEN, and PLANET, and low similarity between FIS and KSS0 (similarity scores were produced for each pair of dimensions and each pair of tools).

AQUINAS also produced several "scatter tables" showing clusters of tools plotted on successive pairs of dimensions. A simplified version of one of these tables, domain independence vs. task class, is shown in Figure 6. The table shows concentrations of interactive knowledge acquisition tools for diagnostic tasks, but the few knowledge acquisition tools

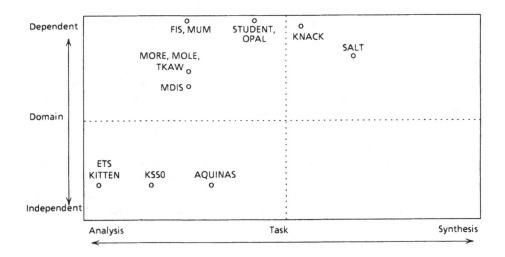

Figure 6. AQUINAS interactive knowledge acquisition tool scatter table for domain independence vs. task class. The table shows concentrations of interactive knowledge acquisition tools for diagnostic tasks, but the few knowledge acquisition tools that exist for synthesis problems are domain-dependent.

that exist for synthesis problems are domain-dependent. Other example tables showed that, generally, it is easier to build automated tools that are more domain-dependent; that, generally, automated knowledge acquisition tools are easier to learn how to use than less automated tools; and that knowledge acquisition tools that support more of the knowledge engineering life cycle tend to be more domain-dependent.

Other patterns in the tools are apparent. For instance, some tools try to draw power using strong specific domain knowledge (FIS, OPAL, MUM); other tools try to address a broader range of problems at the expense of built-in domain-specific problem-solving power (ETS, KITTEN, AQUINAS). The few tools that address synthesis problems are domain dependent. Most researchers seem to be interested in applying their tools to more domain independent and/or harder tasks.

Success in implementing interactive knowledge acquisition tools for particular problems seems to follow success at building large numbers of knowledge-based systems in that domain. Once many systems exist, patterns become apparent that may be exploited by specialized knowledge-based system shells, and in turn, by knowledge acquisition tools. For example, many diagnostic knowledge-based systems exist, specialized diagnostic shells are appearing, and we see a strong concentration of knowledge acquisition tools in this area. As more specific synthesis knowledge-based systems are built and useful specialized shells emerge for these kind of problems, we should expect to see more knowledge acquisition tools for synthesis problems.

2.2. Knowledge Acquisition Workshops and Related Publications

We are attempting to make the knowledge acquisition workshop materials as widely available as possible. The following section details the availability of publications from each workshop and from a new Academic Press knowledge acquisition journal. If you have related questions contact Brian Gaines (gaines@calgary.cdn) or John Boose (john@atc.boeing.com).

First AAAI-Sponsored Knowledge Acquisition for Knowledge-Based Systems Workshop (KAW86), Banff, November 1986
Preprints distributed to attendees only.
Revised and updated papers published in the International Journal of Man-Machine Studies, January, February, April, August, and September 1987 special issues. Papers plus editorial material and index collected in two books in the Knowledge-Based Systems Series: Gaines, B.R. and Boose, J.H. (Eds) Vol. 1: Knowledge Acquisition for Knowledge-Based Systems. London: Academic Press, 1988. Boose, J.H. and Gaines, B.R. (Eds) Vol. 2: Knowledge Acquisition Tools for Expert Systems. London: Academic Press, 1988.

First European Knowledge Acquisition for Knowledge-Based Systems Workshop (EKAW87), Reading, UK, September 1987
Proceedings available as: Proceedings of the First European Workshop on Knowledge Acquisition for Knowledge-Based Systems. Sent sterling money order or draft for 39.00 pounds payable to University of Reading to: Prof. T.R. Addis, Department of Computer Science, University of Reading, Whiteknights, PO Box 220, Reading RG6 2AX, UK.

Second AAAI-Sponsored Knowledge Acquisition for Knowledge-Based Systems Workshop (KAW87), Banff, October 1987
Preprints distributed to attendees only.
Revised and updated papers being published in the International Journal of Man-Machine Studies, 1988 regular issues (August, September, October, November, December, and others). Papers plus editorial material and index will be collected in book form for the Knowledge-Based Systems Series, together with other knowledge acquisition papers from IJMMS. These will be available in Fall, 1989: Gaines, B.R. and Boose, J.H. (Eds) Vol. 3: Machine Learning and Uncertain Reasoning in Knowledge-Based Systems. London: Academic Press, 1989. Boose, J.H. and Gaines, B.R. (Eds) Vol. 4: Knowledge Acquisition: Foundations. London: Academic Press, 1989.

Second European Knowledge Acquisition for Knowledge-Based Systems Workshop (EKAW88), Bonn, West Germany, June 1988
Proceedings available as: Boose, J.H., Gaines, B.R., and Linster, M. (Eds), Proceedings of the European Workshop on Knowledge Acquisition for Knowledge-Based Systems (EKAW88). Send order to (the GMD will invoice you for DM68.00 plus postage): Marc Linster, Institut fur Angewandte Informationstechnik der Gesellschaft fr Mathematik und Datenverarbeitung mbH, Schloss Birlingoven, Postfach 1240, D-5205 Sankt Augustin 1, West Germany.

Third AAAI-Sponsored Knowledge Acquisition for Knowledge-Based Systems Workshop (KAW88), Banff, November 1988
Proceedings/preprints available as: Boose, J.H. and Gaines, B.R. (Eds), Proceedings of the 3rd Knowledge Acquisition for Knowledge-Based Systems Workshop. Send money order, draft, or check drawn on US or Canadian bank for US$65.00 or CDN$85.00 to: SRDG Publications, Department of Computer Science, University of Calgary, Calgary, Alberta, Canada T2N 1N4. Revised and updated papers will be published in the International Journal of Man-Machine Studies, 1989 regular issues, and possibly in the proposed Academic Press journal, Knowledge Acquisition for Knowledge-Based Systems. Papers plus editorial material and index will be collected in book form, together with other knowledge acquisition and related papers from IJMMS and KAKBS in 1990.

Information about proceedings and publications from the workshops below will be available later; get in touch with the listed contact for future information.

Third European Knowledge Acquisition for Knowledge-Based Systems Workshop (EKAW89), Paris, France, July 1989
Contact Jean-Gabriel Ganascia, LAFORIA, Univ. Pierre et Marie Curie, Tour 45–46, 4 Place Jussieu, 75230 Paris Cedex 05; (32)–1–69 41 66 26.

Fourth AAAI-Sponsored Knowledge Acquisition for Knowledge-Based Systems Workshop (KAW89), Banff, October 1–6 1989
Contact Brian Gaines (address above).

Fourth European Knowledge Acquisition for Knowledge-Based Systems Workshop (EKAW90), The Netherlands, Summer, 1990
Contact Bob Wielinga, Department of Social Science Informatics, University of Amsterdam, Herengracht 196, 1016 BS Amsterdam, The Netherlands.

Fifth AAAI-Sponsored Knowledge Acquisition for Knowledge-Based Systems Workshop (KAW90), Fall, 1990
Information about proceedings and publications from this workshop will be available in the future. Contact Brian Gaines (address above).

First Japan Knowledge Acquisition for Knowledge-Based Systems Workshop (JKAW90), Fall, 1990
Contact Hiroshi Motoda, Advanced Research Laboratory, Hitachi, Ltd., Kokubunji, Tokyo 185, Japan.

Journal: *Knowledge Acquisition: An International Journal of Knowledge Acquisition for Knowledge-Based Systems,* Academic Press, Editors: Brian R. Gaines and John H. Boose, first publication in March, 1989.

Aims: Knowledge Acquisition aims to provide those developing knowledge-based systems with access to state-of-the-art research on tools, techniques, methodologies, and foundations for knowledge acquisition from experts, texts, and other sources of human knowledge processes through advanced knowledge-based systems, and particularly on the elicitation and modeling of knowledge in those systems derived from more conventional sources. The emphasis is not on artificial intelligence but on the extension of natural intelligence through knowledge-based systems.

Coverage

Elicitation/modeling of expertise: systems that obtain and model knowledge from experts.
Elicitation/modeling of expertise: manual knowledge acquisition methods and techniques.
Apprenticeship, explanation-based, and other learning systems; integration of such systems with other knowledge acquisition techniques.
Integration of knowledge from multiple experts or other sources; issues in collaborative knowledge-based systems.
Issues in cognition and expertise that affect the knowledge acquisition process.
Extracting and modeling of knowledge from text.
Integration of knowledge acquisition techniques within a single system; integration of knowledge acquisition systems with other systems (hypermedia, database management systems, simulators, spreadsheets).
Knowledge acquisition methodology and training.
Validation of knowledge acquisition techniques; the role of knowledge acquisition techniques in validating knowledge-based systems.

References

Antonelli, D. 1983. The application of artificial intelligence to a maintenance and diagnostic information system (MDIS). *Proceedings of the Joint Services Workshop on Artificial Intelligence in Maintenance.* Boulder, CO.

Boose, J.H. 1984. Personal construct theory and the transfer of human expertise. *Proceedings of the National Conference on Artificial Intelligence* (AAAI-84), p. 27–33, Austin, Texas.

Boose, J.H. 1985. A knowledge acquisition program for expert systems based on personal construct psychology. *International Journal of Man-Machine Studies, 23,* 495–525.

Boose, J.H. 1986a. *Expertise Transfer for Expert System Design,* New York: Elsevier.

Boose, J.H. 1986b. Rapid acquisition and combination of knowledge from multiple experts in the same domain. *Future Computing Systems Journal, 1,* 191–216.

Boose, J.H. 1988. Uses of repertory grid-centred knowledge acquisition tools for knowledge-based systems. *International Journal of Man-Machine Studies, 29,* 287–310.

Boose, J.H. 1989. A survey of knowledge acquisition techniques and tools. *Knowledge acquisition: An international journal of knowledge acquisition for knowledge-based systems,* in press, Vol. 1, No. 1.

Boose, J.H., and Bradshaw, J.M. 1987a. Expertise transfer and complex problems: using Aquinas as a knowledge acquisition workbench for expert systems. Special issue on the 1st Knowledge Acquisition for Knowledge-Based Systems Workshop, 1986, Part 1, *International Journal of Man-Machine Studies, 26,* 3–28; also in Boose, J.H., and Gaines, B.R. (eds), *Knowledge-based systems Vol. 2: Knowledge acquisition tools for expert systems.* New York: Academic Press, 1988.

Boose, J.H., and Bradshaw, J.M. 1987b. AQUINAS: A knowledge acquisition workbench for building knowledge-based systems. *Proceedings of the First European Workshop on Knowledge Acquisition for Knowledge-Based Systems* (pp. A6.1–6). Reading University.

Boose, J.H., Bradshaw, J.M., Shema, D.B. 1988. Recent progress in Aquinas: A knowledge acquisition workbench. *Proceedings of the Second European Knowledge Acquisition Workshop* (EKAW-88). p. 2.1–15, Bonn.

Bradshaw, J. 1988. Shared causal knowledge as a basis for communication between expert and knowledge acquisition system. *Proceedings of the Second European Knowledge Acquisition Workshop (EKAW-88)* pp. 12.1–6.

Bradshaw, J.M. 1988. Strategies for selecting and interviewing experts. Boeing Computer Services Technical report, in preparation.

Bradshaw, J.M., and Boose, J.H. 1989. Decision analytic techniques for knowledge acquisition: Combining situation and preference models using Aquinas. Special issue on the 2nd Knowledge Acquisition for Knowledge-Based Systems Workshop, 1987, *International Journal of Man-Machine Studies,* in press.

Clancey, W. 1986. Heuristic classification. In J. Kowalik (Ed.). *Knowledge-based problem-solving.* New York: Prentice-Hall.

Davis, R., and Lenat, D.B. 1982. *Knowledge-based systems in artificial intelligence.* New York: McGraw-Hill.

DeJong, K. 1987. Knowledge acquisition for fault isolation expert systems. Special issue on the 1st AAAI Knowledge Acquisition for Knowledge-Based Systems Workshop, 1986, Part 4, *International Journal of Man-Machine Studies,* Vol. 27, No. 2.

Eshelman, L, Ehret, D., McDermott, J., and Tan, M. 1987. MOLE: A tenacious knowledge acquisition tool. Special issue on the 1st AAAI Knowledge Acquisition for Knowledge-Based Systems Workshop, 1986, Part 1, *International Journal of Man-Machine Studies, 26,* 41–54; also in Boose, J.H., and Gaines, B.R. (Eds), *Knowledge-based systems Vol. 2: Knowledge acquisition tools for expert systems,* New York: Academic Press, 1988.

Eshelman, L. 1988. MOLE: A knowledge acquisition tool that buries certainty factors. Special issue on the 2nd Knowledge Acquisition for Knowledge-Based Systems Workshop, 1987, *International Journal of Man-Machine Studies,* in press.

Gaines, B.R. 1987a. An overview of knowledge acquisition and transfer. Special issue on the 1st Knowledge Acquisition for Knowledge-Based Systems Workshop, 1986, Part 3, *International Journal of Man-Machine Studies, 26,* 453–472; also in B.R. Gaines and J.H. Boose (Eds), *Knowledge-based systems Vol. 1: Knowledge acquisition for knowledge-based systems.* New York: Academic Press.

Gaines, B.R. 1987b. Knowledge acquisition for expert systems. *Proceedings of the First European Workshop on Knowledge Acquisition for Knowledge-Based Systems,* (pp. A3.1–4). Reading, University.

Gaines, B.R. 1988a. Advanced expert system support environments. Special issue on the 2nd Knowledge Acquisition for Knowledge-Based Systems Workshop, 1987, *International Journal of Man-Machine Studies,* in press.

Gaines, B.R. 1988b. Second generation knowledge acquisition systems. *Proceedings of the Second European Knowledge Acquisition Workshop (EKAW-88)*, (pp. 17.1–14). Bonn.

Gaines, B.R., and Boose, J.H. 1989. A summary of the AAAI-sponsored knowledge acquisition for knowledge-based system workshops. *AI Magazine*, in press.

Gaines, B.R. and Sharp, M. 1987. A knowledge acquisition extension to notecards. *Proceedings of the First European Workshop on Knowledge Acquisition for Knowledge-Based Systems*, (pp. C1.1–7). Reading University.

Gruber, T.R., Cohen, P.R. 1987. Design for acquisition: Principles of knowledge system design to facilitate knowledge acquisition. Special issue on the 1st Knowledge Acquisition for Knowledge-Based Systems Workshop, 1986, Part 2, *International Journal of Man-Machine Studies, 26*, 143–160; also in J.H. Boose and B.R. Gaines (Eds), *Knowledge-based systems Vol. 2: Knowledge acquisition tools for expert systems*. New York: Academic Press.

Kahn, G., Nowlan, S., and McDermott, J. 1985a. Strategies for knowledge acquisition. *IEEE Transactions of Pattern Analysis and Machine Intelligence*, PAMI-7 (3), 511–522.

Kahn, G., Nowlan, S., and McDermott, J. 1985b. MORE: An intelligent knowledge acquisition tool. *Proceedings of the Ninth Joint Conference on Artificial Intelligence*, (pp. 581–584). Los Angeles, CA.

Kahn, G.S., Breaux, E.H., Joeseph, R.L., and DeKlerk, P. 1987. An intelligent mixed-initiative workbench for knowledge acquisition. Special issue on the 1st AAAI Knowledge Acquisition for Knowledge-Based Systems Workshop, 1986, Part 4, *International Journal of Man-Machine Studies, 27*, 167–180; also in J.H. Boose and B.R. Gaines (Eds), *Knowledge-based systems Vol.2: Knowledge acquisition tools for expert systems*. New York: Academic Press.

Kitto, C.M., and Boose, J.H. 1987. Heuristics for expertise transfer: The automatic management of complex knowledge acquisition dialogs. Special issue on the 1st Knowledge Acquisition for Knowledge-Based Systems Workshop, 1986, Part 2, *International Journal of Man-Machine Studies, 26*, 183–202; also in J.H. Boose and B.R. Gaines (Eds), *Knowledge-based systems Vol. 2: Knowledge acquisition tools for expert systems*. New York: Academic Press.

Kitto, C.M., and Boose, J.H. 1988. Selecting knowledge acquisition tools and strategies based on application characteristics. Special issues on the 2nd Knowledge Acquisition for Knowledge-Based Systems Workshop, 1987, *International Journal of Man-Machine Studies*, in press.

Klinker, G., Bentolila, J., Genetet, S., Grimes, M., and McDermott, J. 1987. KNACK: Report-driven knowledge acquisition. Special issue on the 1st AAAI Knowledge Acquisition for Knowledge-Based Systems Workshop, 1986, Part 1, *International Journal of Man-Machine Studies, 26*, 65–80; also in J.H. Boose and B.R. Gaines (Eds), *Knowledge-based systems Vol. 2: Knowledge acquisition tools for expert systems*. New York: Academic Press.

Klinker, G., Genetet, S., and McDermott, J. 1988. Knowledge acquisition for evaluation systems. Special issue on the 2nd Knowledge Acquisition for Knowledge-Based Systems Workshop, 1987, *International Journal of Man-Machine Studies*, in press.

Marcus, S., McDermott, J., and Wang, T. 1985. Knowledge acquisition for constructive systems. *Proceedings of the Ninth Joint Conference on Artificial Intelligence*, (pp. 637–639). Los Angeles, CA.

Marcus, S. 1987. Taking backtracking with a grain of SALT. Special issue on the 1st Knowledge Acquisition for Knowledge-Based Systems Workshop, 1986, Part 3, *International Journal of Man-Machine Studies, 26*, 383–398; also in J.H. Boose and B.R. Gaines (Eds), *Knowledge-based systems Vol. 2: Knowledge acquisition tools for expert systems*. New York: Academic Press.

Musen, M.A., Fagan, L.M., Combs, D.M., and Shortliffe, E.H. 1987. Use of domain model to drive an interactive knowledge-editing tool. Special issue on the 1st AAAI Knowledge Acquisition for Knowledge-Based Systems Workshop, 1986, Part 1, *International Journal of Man-Machine Studies, 26*, 105–121; also in J.H. Boose and B.R. Gaines (Eds), *Knowledge-based systems Vol. 2: Knowledge acquisition tools for expert systems*. New York: Academic Press.

Shaw, M.L.G. 1988. Problems of validation in a knowledge acquisition system using multiple experts. *Proceedings of the Second European Knowledge Acquisition Workshop (EKAW-88)*, (pp 5.1–15). Bonn.

Shaw, M.L.G., and Gaines, B.R. 1987. Techniques for knowledge acquisition and transfer. Special issue on the 1st Knowledge Acquisition for Knowledge-Based Systems Workshop, 1986, Part 5 , *International Journal of Man-Machine Studies, 27*, 251–280.

Shaw. M.L.G., and Woodward, J.B. 1988. Validation in a knowledge support system: Construing consistency with multiple experts. Special issue on the 2nd Knowledge Acquisition for Knowledge-Based Systems Workshop, 1987, *International Journal of Man-Machine Studies, 29*, 329–350.

Shema, D.B., and Boose, J.H. 1988. Refining problem-solving knowledge in repertory grids using a consultation mechanism. Special issue on the 2nd Knowledge Acquisition for Knowledge-Based Systems Workshop, 1987, *International Journal of Man-Machine Studies,* 447–460.

Stout, J., Caplain, G., Marcus, S., and McDermott, J. 1988. Toward automating recognition of differing problem-solving demands. Special issue on the 2nd Knowledge Acquisition for Knowledge-Based Systems Workshop, 1987, *International Journal of Man-Machine Studies,* in press.

Table of Contents: Volume 4 (1989)

INDEX

Automating Knowledge Acquisition for Expert Systems

Edited by **Sandra Marcus,** *Boeing Computer Services*

Automating Knowledge Acquisition for Expert Systems describes a set of studies in automating knowledge acquisition. The studies create tools and methodologies designed to reduce the cost of building and maintaining expert systems.

The tools discussed in this book are useful working models for expert systems. They are applicable to a range of tasks, and can be used to support multiple applications. The book's approach to creating tools can be used to make any system more accessible and maintainable. **Automating Knowledge Acquisition for Expert Systems** is oriented toward practical uses of AI and will be of interest to people who have some experience with building expert systems.

Contents
Preface* Introduction* MORE: From Observing Knowledge Engineers to Automating Knowledge Acquisition* MOLE: A Knowledge-Acquisition Tool for Cover-and-Differentiate Systems* SALT: A Knowledge-Acquisition Tool for Propose-and-Revise Systems* KNACK: Sample-Driven Knowledge Acquisition for Reporting Systems* SIZZLE: A Knowledge-Acquisition Tool Specialized for the Sizing Task* RIME: Preliminary Work Toward a Knowledge Acquisition Tool* Preliminary Steps Toward a Taxonomy of Problem-Solving Methods* Index

1988 ISBN 0-89838-286-6   Cloth   224pp. $57.50   Dfl. 130.00 £34.50

The Authors...

Sandra Marcus, *Boeing Computer Services*

Judith Bachant, *Digital Equipment Corp.*
Gary Kahn, *Carnegie Group Inc.*
John McDermott, *Digital Equipment Corp.*

Larry Eshelman, *Philips Laboratories*
Georg Klinker, *Digital Equipment Corp.*
Daniel Offut, *University of Michigan*

Kluwer
Academic
P U B L I S H E R S
Order Department, P.O. Box 358
Accord Station, Hingham, MA 02018-0358

Orders Outside the U.S. and Canada:
KLUWER ACADEMIC PUBLISHERS
Distribution Center
P.O. Box 322
3300 AH Dordrecht
The Netherlands

Machine Learning, Meta-Reasoning and Logics

Edited by **Pavel B. Brazdil**, *University of Porto*
and **Kurt Konolige**, *SRI International*

Learning, representation and reasoning have all been examined by AI researchers in isolation, but a workshop held in Sesimbra, Portugal during February of 1988 approached the three with a comprehensive view of their overlap and interactions. This book is an outgrowth of selected papers from the workshop.

Contents

Preface* Acknowledgments* Introduction* Meta-Reasoning and Machine Learning* Reasoning about Proofs and Explanations* Foundations of AI and Machine Learning

1990   ISBN 0-7923-9047-4   Cloth
352pp. $65.00   £ 45.25   Dfl. 165.00

Change of Representation and Inductive Bias

Edited by **D. Paul Benjamin**, *Philips Laboratories*

Change of Representation and Inductive Bias is the first collection of papers on representation change, a topic of growing importance in the fields of machine learning and knowledge representation. The book is based on CRIB '88, the first international gathering of researchers on this topic.

Contributors

David W. Aha* Ranan Banerji* D. Paul Benjamin* Wesley Braudaway* Nicholas Flann* Benjamin N. Grosof* Haym Hirsh* Robert Holte* Dennis Kibler* Craig Knoblock* Mieczyslaw M. Kokar* Michael Lowry* Larry Rendell* Patricia Riddle* Stuart Russell* Jeff Schlimmer* Devika Subramanian* Josh D. Tenenberg* Wlodek W. Zadrozny* R. M. Zimmer

1990   ISBN 0-7923-9055-5   Cloth   354pp.
Price to be announced

Learning Search Control Knowledge: An Explanation-Based Approach

By **Steven Minton**, *Carnegie Mellon University*

Contents

Introduction*Analyzing the Utility Problem*Overview of the PRODIGY Problem Solver* Specialization*Compression*Utility Evaluation*Learning from Success*Learning from Failure* Learning from Goal Interactions*Performance Results*Proofs, Explanations and Correctness: Putting It All Together*Related Work*Conclusion*Appendix I: Domain Specifications*Index

1988   ISBN 0-89838-294-7   Cloth   224pp. $49.95   £ 31.95   Dfl. 120.00

Kluwer
Academic
P U B L I S H E R S
Order Department, P.O. Box 358
Accord Station, Hingham, MA 02018-0358

Orders Outside the U.S. and Canada:
KLUWER ACADEMIC PUBLISHERS
Distribution Center
P.O. Box 322
3300 AH Dordrecht
The Netherlands